Scott Cohen's
Poolscapes

Photo by Paul Jonason

Scott Cohen's
Poolscapes

Refreshing Ideas for the Ultimate Backyard Resort

Schiffer Publishing Ltd

4880 Lower Valley Road, Atglen, Pennsylvania 19310

Photographers:

Nick Lucero, Deidra Walpole, Paul C. Jonason,
Scott Cohen, Patrick Stringer, Jose Hernandez

Resources and Contributors:

All projects design by Scott Cohen and built by
The Green Scene
19431 Londelius St., Northridge, CA 91324
(818) 280-0420

ScottCohenDesigns.com, GreenSceneLandscape.com,
Fetch-A-Sketch.com, OutdoorKitchenDesignIdeas.com,
AwardWinningPools.com

Other Schiffer Books on Related Subjects:
Creating Ponds, Brooks, and Pools. Ulrich Timm. ISBN: 0764309153.
   $29.95.
International Award-winning Pools, Spas and Water Environments.
   Virginia Martino, Joseph M. Vassallo, & Mary Vail. ISBN:
   9780764334801. $24.99
*Natural Swimming Pools: An Inspirational Guide for Construction
   and Maintenance.* Michael Littlewood FLI, FSGD. ISBN:
   0764321838. $49.95

Original Design by Jose Hernandez, Marie NyBlom
Modified by Mark David Bowyer
Type set in Hallmarke Black / Humanist521BT

ISBN: 978-0-7643-3740-6
Printed in China

Schiffer Books are available at special discounts for bulk purchases
for sales promotions or premiums. Special editions, including
personalized covers, corporate imprints, and excerpts can be
created in large quantities for special needs. For more information
contact the publisher:

Published by Schiffer Publishing Ltd.
4880 Lower Valley Road
Atglen, PA 19310
Phone: (610) 593-1777; Fax: (610) 593-2002
E-mail: Info@schifferbooks.com

For the largest selection of fine reference books on this and
related subjects, please visit our web site at
www.schifferbooks.com

We are always looking for people to write books on new and
related subjects. If you have an idea for a book
please contact us at the above address.

This book may be purchased from the publisher.
Include $5.00 for shipping.
Please try your bookstore first.
You may write for a free catalog.
In Europe, Schiffer books are distributed by
Bushwood Books
6 Marksbury Ave.
Kew Gardens
Surrey TW9 4JF England
Phone: 44 (0) 20 8392 8585; Fax: 44 (0) 20 8392 9876
E-mail: info@bushwoodbooks.co.uk
Website: www.bushwoodbooks.co.uk

Contents

Find Your Dream

What's the ultimate backyard pool? Is it a cozy, romantic getaway for two or a splashy playground for family fun? Is it the neighborhood "Party Central" or a place to escape and unwind? A tropical lagoon? A woodland meadow? A soothing oasis in an exotic, faraway land?

It all depends … on you.

For me, the ultimate poolscape is one that truly reflects the tastes, passions, and lifestyle of the people I created it for. As a designer, my goal is to get inside the heads of my clients, to discover what brings them joy, what moves them and what makes them laugh.

Hobbies, travel, personality traits—all of these go into the mix as I create a design with one person, one couple or one family in mind. I may test ideas and work with different concepts, but I always know when I hit the target with a design that dazzles their senses.

Throughout the construction process, my team and I continuously stay in touch with our clients' needs, wishes, and sense of style. We respond with unique details woven into every aspect of the project.

When it's complete, there's nothing I enjoy more than showing my clients the unique environment we've created just for them. I'll be honest; I'm usually as blown away by the results as they are. I can say that with all humility because these special places are always the product of a team effort between my clients, my staff, and me.

I hope you enjoy this tour of twenty-five of my favorite pool and spa projects. Along the way, I'll share some of the tips and tricks I've learned so you can use them in your own backyard design.

Most of all, I hope you can share in the fun my clients and I had in making these dreams reality. (When I was young, I spent a lot of time playing with Legos. The bricks are a lot bigger and heavier now, but it's still the same game and I love playing it.)

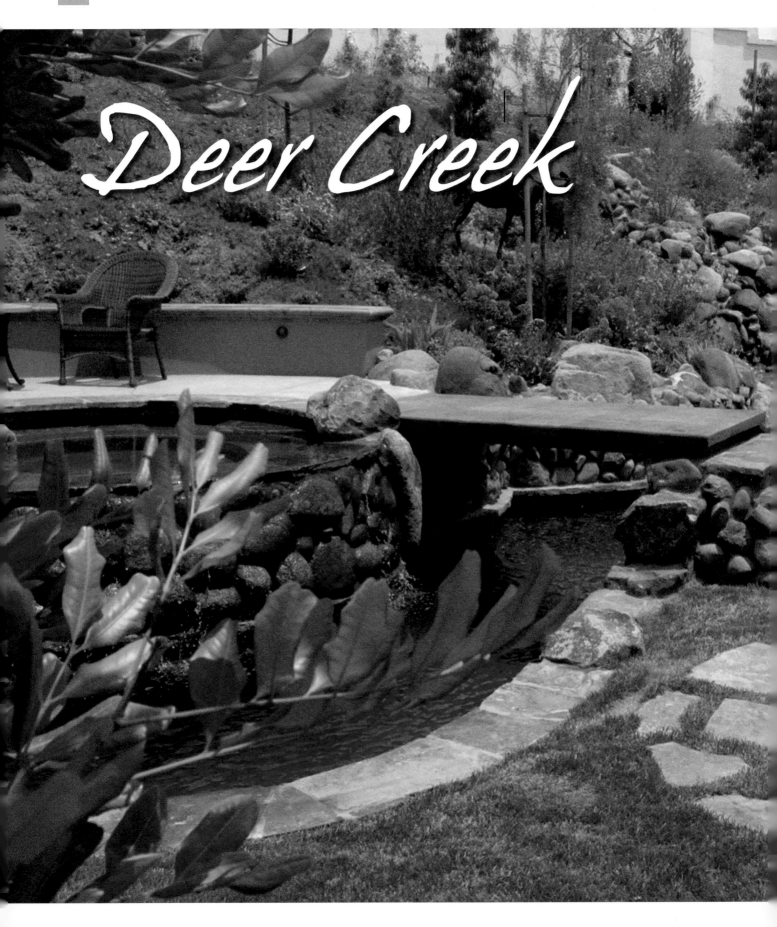

Deer Creek

Deer Creek

Who needs a lap pool when there's a deep, clear, inviting creek right outside the door? In this backyard, a small stream tumbles down the hillside into the refreshing pool below. Two deer look up to see who's visiting their quiet home.

The clients for this project wanted all the functionality of a lap pool with the appeal of a secluded natural creek. To meet their needs, we created this multi-tiered waterfall and free-form pool with a 50 foot swim-line perfect for morning exercise. Cobblestone, flagstone, faux stone, and trailing wildflowers all add authenticity to this babbling backyard brook. Après swim, bathers can soak up the sun on the Baja shelf, slip into the bubbling spa, or warm up by the stone fire-pit.

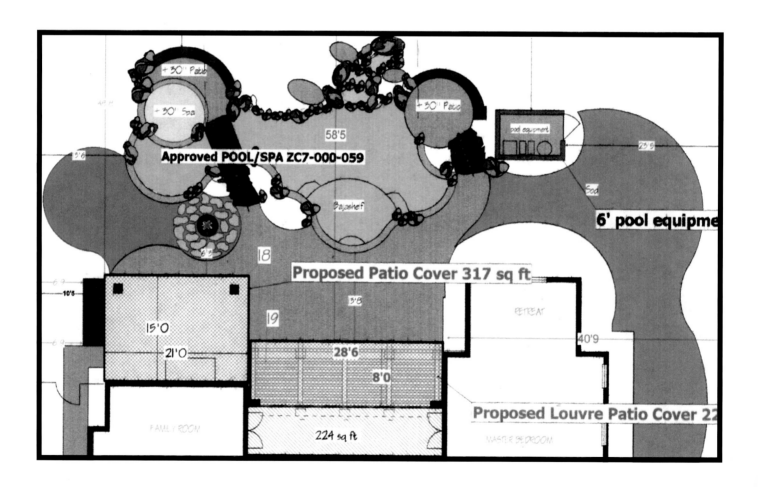

Fetch-A-Sketch.com

To maximize space in this challenging sloped yard we raised the rear bond beam of the pool. With the pool wall serving as a retaining wall, the raised bistro patio, spa, and pool all tuck neatly into the hillside. A stamped concrete "wooden" bridge leads to the spa.

The large bronze deer are anchored on concrete footings but seem to step right out of the woods, adding another naturalistic detail to the scene. The Baja shelf (aka a "sun shelf"), with ample room for two lounge chairs, makes a perfect spot for side-by-side sunbathing.

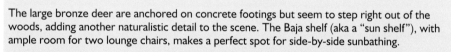

The pool was finished with natural pebbles in a deep pacific blue. Colored glass fish tiles adorn the pool walls and sparkle in the sunlight.

Patios were created with stone textured stamped concrete in a sandstone color.

This yard was recently filmed by the Concrete Network for use as an example of the epitome of outdoor room design. Flagstone bands and steps add natural accents.

Design Tips :

Reflect: The wide spillway offers a generous reflective surface as water cascades from spa to pool. Placement of the fire pit near the spa allows the water to capture the reflection of the flames and keeps couples warm in or out of the water.

Branch Out: A waterfall that splits into two or three channels looks much more natural than one that follows a single path.

Room to Relax: Many homeowners prefer a Baja shelf over the slant of a zero-entry pool, which can make lounging difficult. The shelf's level expanse makes it easy to kick back and cool off in comfort.

Up and Out: Break up your outdoor space into different patio areas at varying levels. Take advantage of the height as well as the horizontal space to create additional outdoor rooms. The raised seating area behind the spa adds even more space to this sloped yard. The bridge's 30" rise over the water gives a comfortable reach for swimmers passing underneath.

No Pressure: When using a pool wall as a retaining wall, make sure you include a hydrostatic release drain behind it and make sure the pool wall is waterproofed to prevent moisture from wicking through.

Stamp It: Stamped concrete offers the aesthetics of wood with less maintenance, superior slip resistance, and no splinters.

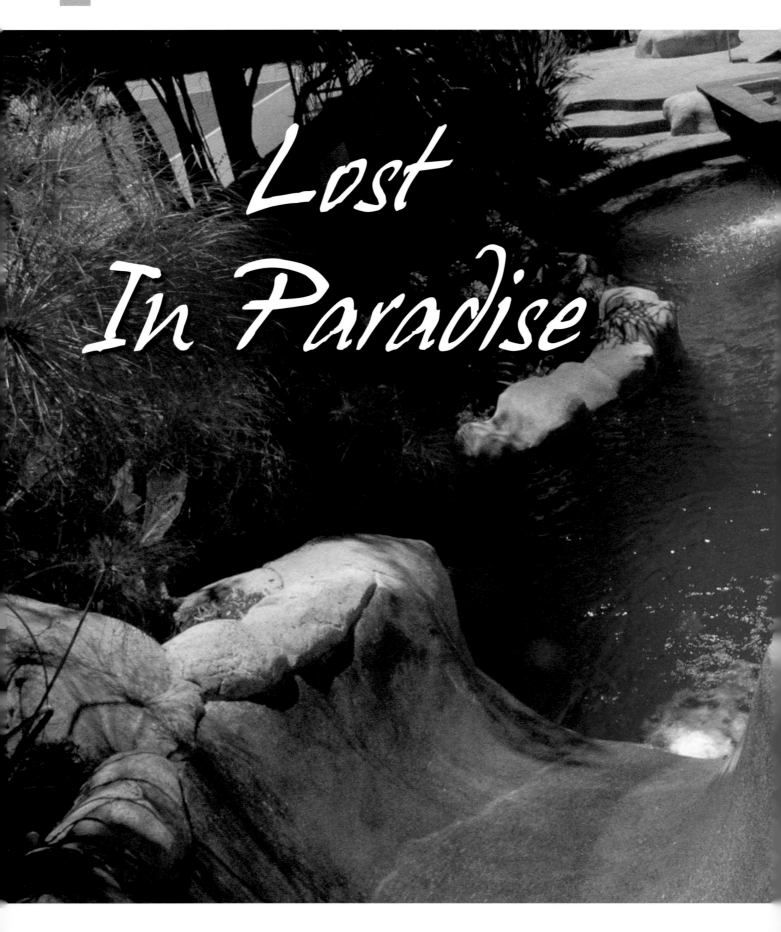

Lost
In Paradise

Lost In Paradise

Do you ever dream about being stranded on a beautiful deserted island?

We made that dream come true for one young family with this playful backyard. Story has it they were all out boating one day when they ran aground on some rocks. Now they're a family of castaways, having one adventure after another on this private island paradise.

The clients wanted a "Robinson Crusoe" themed pool that would guarantee family fun with their three kids. They also wanted a romantic escape for the parents when the little pirates go to bed. To create this fantasy, we designed a boat-shaped spa "on-the-rocks." Water inundates the boat and a leak from the impact sprays into the large free-form pool. We added a "wooden" concrete dock and a twenty-foot slide with a cave underneath, perfect for hiding (and finding) buried treasure. There's even a palapa and a sandy beach that doubles as a sand-trap for the adjacent putting green. Palm trees, boulders, and lush tropical plantings complete the story.

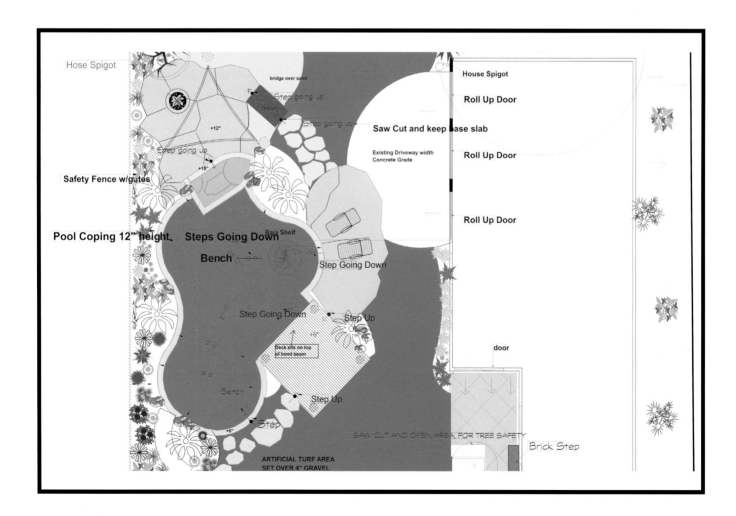

Fetch-A-Sketch.com

The slide and rocks are all faux rock work that was manufactured and carved on site. To create the boat spa, we made forms using flexible faux wood textured house-siding panels and used acid staining to mimic the look of weathered planks. Like any ship aground, the water-filled boat lists a bit, spilling into the pool to create a whimsical water feature.

A faux wood stamped concrete bridge leads to the raised patio adjacent to the spa. During the day, the palapa, thatched with Bali-imported palm, offers cooling shade from the tropical sun. At night, the fire pit serves as a great place for island explorers to gather and share stories.

(Fortunately, the family was able to salvage a lifetime supply of marshmallows before the boat sank.) The dock patio was made with wood-textured stamped concrete. Wood posts and nautical rope enhance the illusion. Stamped concrete pads lead from pool to slide.

An outdoor kitchen includes a cast concrete counter embedded with seashells, fossils and other island treasures. This sinking boat is actually a hydrotherapy spa with a well in the bow deep enough for one or two weary castaways to stand in. Bench jets along the sides, foot jets on the floor, and soothing jets up and down the well create a relaxing, romantic sanctuary at the end of the day.

A large Baja shelf allows ample room for two to catch some rays while the pop-up fountain is cooling fun for pirates at play.

Design Tips :

Break up backyard space into outdoor rooms using various elevations, materials, and finishes interspersed with plantings.

Raised spas create a natural water-feature as water spills over the edge and take advantage of the energy being used by the circulation pump daily.

Use free-form shapes to achieve a tropical effect.

For safety, allow five feet on either side of a slide and a minimum of 15 feet in front.

If using artificial turf, include concrete pads in walking areas. Though artificial turf saves water and maintenance, it can be uncomfortably hot in summer.

When staining cast concrete with acid chemicals, neutralize with baking soda before sealing or colors will continue to darken.

Design Notes :

Due to family allergies, artificial turf was used throughout the project offering an attractive, low-maintenance backdrop.

The pool sports a pebble finish in Tahoe blue. Pool coping is stamped concrete with a faux rock texture.

Blue Lagoon

Photo by Paul Jonason

Blue Lagoon

A misty Hawaiian waterfall and tranquil swimming lagoon provide the inspiration for this tropical getaway. Water cascades over the rocks into a deep grotto pool below. Behind the falls, a hidden slide plunges through the spray into the cool water.

The goal of this project was to provide a romantic, relaxing sanctuary for parents in a backyard that was fun and kid-friendly too. To create this hidden rainforest stream, we crafted a 20' X 30' naturalistic free-form pool and an 8' X 10' deep-well hydrotherapy spa surrounded by boulders, palm trees, and luxuriant plantings. Bathers in the spa enjoy two soothing styles of warm massage from separate streams of heated water. One flows smoothly over the shoulders while the other descends with choppy turbulence. Misters embedded in the stonework add a realistic detail and offer a cooling touch on hot days.

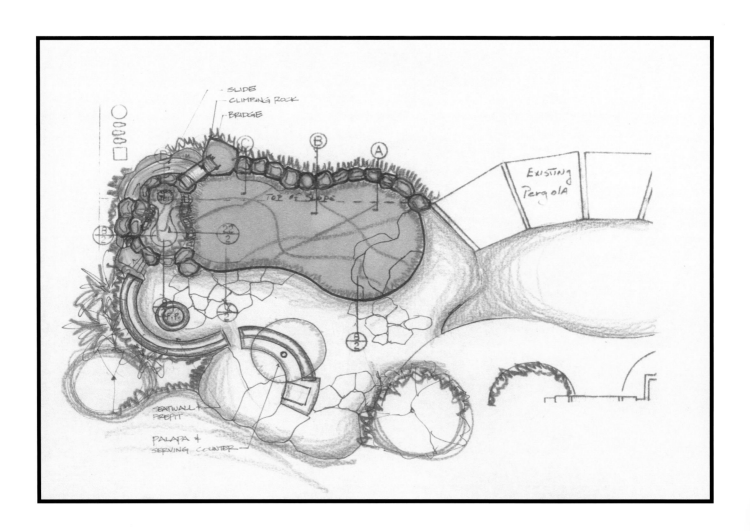

Photo by Paul Jonason

The pool uses a free-standing design with one wall serving as a large retaining wall that extends downward at the back of the property. Palm trees grow from within this ten-foot wall. The ladder climbs the faux-rock boulders then drops down into a slide running through a cave hidden behind the spa.

At the bottom of the slide, a waterfall rains down from above giving swimmers a splash before they take the plunge. On the other side of the spa, a cast concrete bench surrounds a colorful cast concrete fire pit and bar that were cast in place with concrete, embedded glass chips, and fiber optic lights. The fire pit is filled with colored glass, and the bar has a custom rope edge.

Photos by Paul Jonason

This backyard has grown with the family. New additions include a rock climbing wall with embedded hand-holds and a faux wood stamped concrete diving bridge

Tiki torches and a Tiki bar complete this backyard resort.

Rocks and boulders double as planters that blend seamlessly into the tropical scene. The pool deck is made of flagstone and stamped stone textured concrete.

Design Tips :

Natural Variations: When designing with faux rocks, be sure to use a variety of heights, shapes, textures, and jointing for realistic detail.

Mix It Up: Variety adds authenticity to tropical themed plantings as well. Add depth using plants with large leaves, variegated coloring, and diverse textures. Include palms under-planted with giant bird-of-paradise, tropical canna and calla lilies.

Add Curves: Use a curvy free-form pool for a more naturalistic landscape.

Sound Advice: When designing an outdoor sound system, use multiple small speakers rather than two large ones. Numerous speakers placed throughout the garden create ambient sound that can be turned down, allowing for conversation and a more resort-like feel.

Mister Maintenance: Misting systems need adequate filtration and should be cleaned once a month to prevent clogging.

Oasis With A Twist

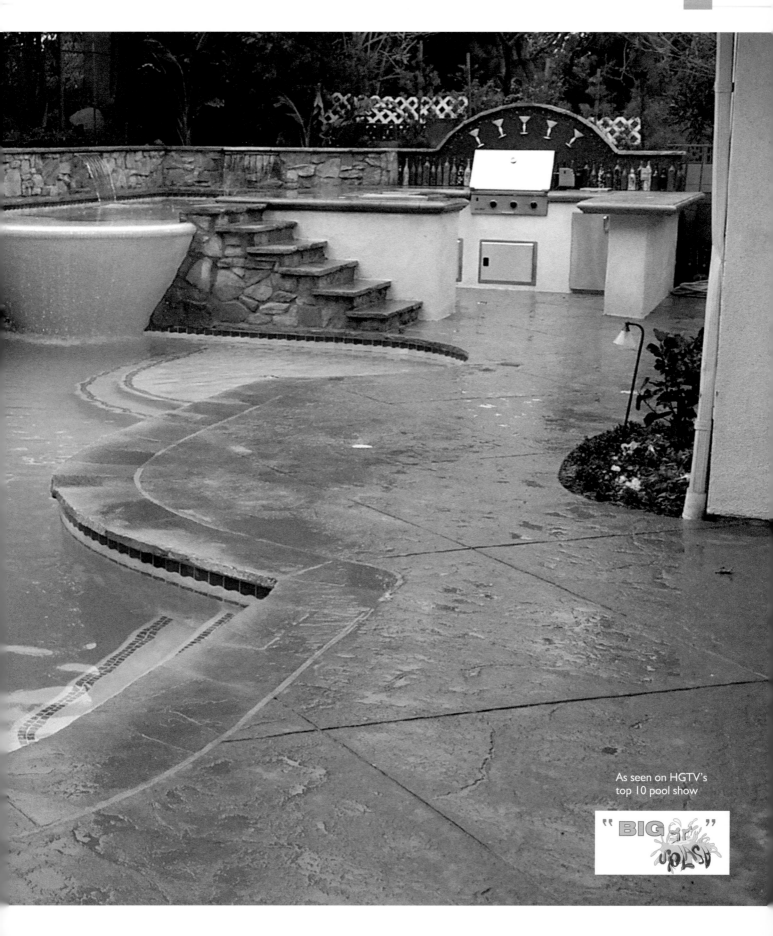

As seen on HGTV's
top 10 pool show

"BIG SPLASH"

Oasis With A Twist

"I'll have a spa with a twist, please." In this entertaining backyard, a martini-shaped spa spills into the pool and festive cocktail glasses dance above a row of colorful ceramic bottles.

The clients wanted an exciting backyard for family and friends of all ages. Because they enjoy a good martini, I originally threw out this martini-themed concept in jest, but it quickly evolved into a real-life cocktail of whimsical fun. The martini glass is deep enough to allow bathers to stand in a hydro-therapy tube that morphs with the flip of a valve from jets that pulsate up and down the body, to a whirling vortex pool, so bathers can choose from either "shaken" or "stirred." An eight-foot-long swim-up bar adjacent to the outdoor kitchen makes a splash-happy place for cook and company. While he's keeping an eye on the burgers, the chef can deal a hand of blackjack with waterproof cards.

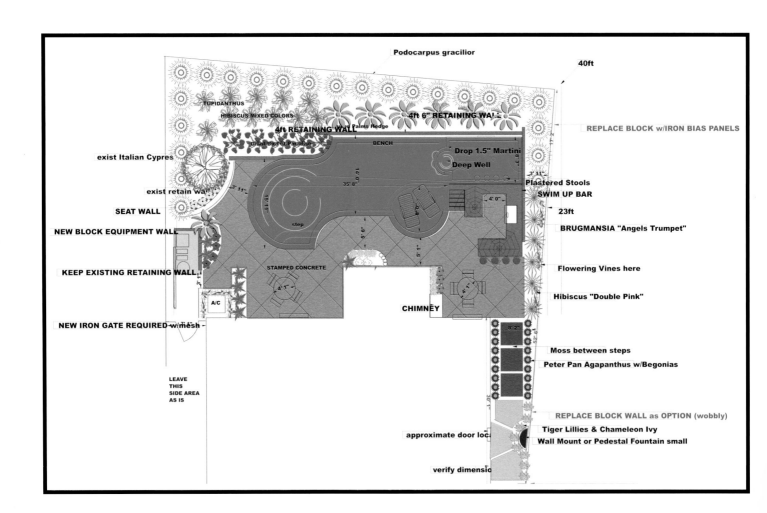

Fetch-A-Sketch.com

In this small yard we were challenged to pack a lot of features into a very small space. Raising the back wall (bond beam) enabled us to cut into the slope and carve out enough area for the pool, spa, patios, and outdoor kitchen, and also allows for easy access for climbing up and jumping into this kid-friendly pool.

The spa is crafted with 1x1 opalescent tiles that sparkle with a pearly luminescence when they catch the sun.

The swim-up bar includes four built-in stools, each adorned with a hand-made martini glass tile. Water spilling from the back wall creates an entertaining feature and aids in circulation. The spillways in the spa allow for heated over the shoulder massage.

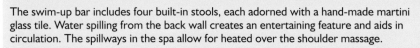

To cast the back-splash, I secretly "borrowed" a martini glass from the clients' set to make a mold. I used real olives to make plaster molds for the olive accent tiles. The colorful ceramic bottles were cast from wine and spirit bottles, then hand-glazed by each member of the family.

Kids have a blast lounging on the shallow lip of the "glass" or sliding over the edge into the pool.

The kitchen counter is cast concrete and the steps to the spa are flagstone.

Raising the height of the spa to 36 inches allowed us to cut further into the hill. Since this brought it up to standard counter height, it offered a natural place for a swim-up bar.

Design Tips :

• Adding aggregate to the plaster mix will double the life of the plaster and improve its performance.

• A darker plaster finish will allow the pool to absorb more sunlight and keep it warmer using less energy.

• When building a swim-up bar, use a bond breaker between the bond beam and the cantilevered swim-up counter to prevent cracking. We use neoprene to allow flexibility between the two units and allow for potential movement.

• Mixing coordinating finishes like natural stone with stone-textured concrete offers unlimited design flexibility.

• In small backyards, think out of the box. If you can't build further out, you might gain additional space with changes in elevation.

Design Notes :

The pool is finished with flagstone coping and coated in white plaster mixed with blue 3M Colorquartz Crystals. These bits of ceramic-coated aggregate act like tiny tiles, protecting the plaster and deepening the color.

This pool was featured on the HGTV special *Big Splash*, a countdown of America's top ten backyard pools. The new yard allowed ample space for entertaining the Chumash Swimbash, an annual YMCA ritual.

The patios are made of stamped stone-textured concrete. I like to use one base color and at least two release colors to add richness and depth.

Sanctuary in the City

Photo by Deidra Walpole

Sanctuary in the City

Where would you rather spend the day? In a hot residential backyard surrounded by neighbors or relaxing under the shade in a quiet Tuscan estate?

In this project, sophisticated old-world styling transformed a typical urban backyard into an elegant escape in the Italian countryside. This property backs up to four other houses on each side. To help the client find privacy in this fishbowl, I designed this Tuscan-inspired garden enclosed in greenery and stonework. Along one side of the yard, a hedge of fern pine and a vine-covered arbor provide two layers of screening and create a colorful backdrop for the pool. An outdoor living room anchored with a generously-sized stone fireplace enhances the sense of privacy. Carefully placed water features create a pool reminiscent of a Roman bath. The flowing water helps hush city sounds with its refreshing sound.

We notched the back of the pool to make room for the columns and create an interesting and elegant shape. This also enabled us to continue the line from kitchen to living-room and pool for a smooth integration of these outdoor rooms.

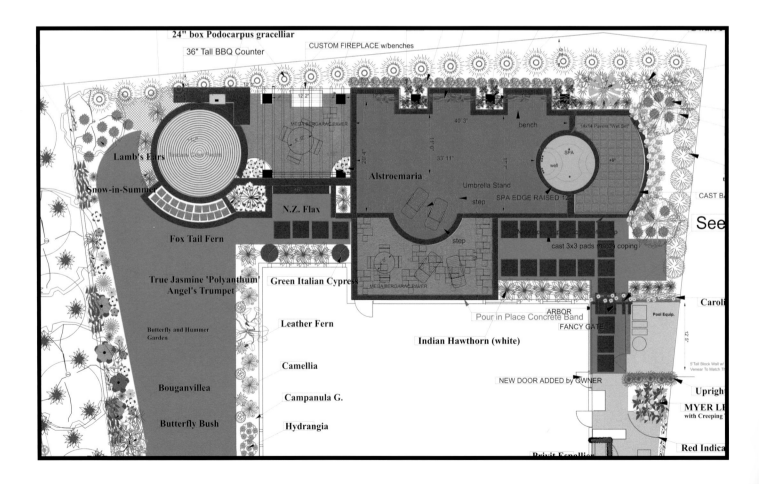

Fetch-A-Sketch.com

Water spills from hand-carved stone weirs in an oversized spa into the pool. Weirs are typically made of copper, stainless, or clay but stone added a level of authenticity to this project. We used a tile saw and grinder to carve each one, making sure they were identically shaped for an even flow of water. Concrete pavers around the spa and large stone-textured concrete stepping pads leave room for grass. This refined look keeps the area cool and green while defining pathways.

Tuscan style columns support the arbor. The columns are repeated in the living-room pergola to unite these spaces.

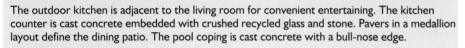

The outdoor kitchen is adjacent to the living room for convenient entertaining. The kitchen counter is cast concrete embedded with crushed recycled glass and stone. Pavers in a medallion layout define the dining patio. The pool coping is cast concrete with a bull-nose edge.

Photos by Deidra Walpole

A butterfly garden, elevated container plantings, topiary, and planters at the base of the arbor add color at all levels and help create that Italian summer feel.

We created the side patio with cast concrete hand-seeded with exposed aggregate. The exposed aggregate is repeated in the outdoor living room.

Design Tips :

Seamless Transitions: To differentiate patio spaces, treat each outdoor room with distinct flooring materials. Bring them together in one cohesive design by coordinating colors and repeating key shapes, patterns, and materials.

Pattern Perfect: A circle pack kit of pavers such as the one by Belgard used for the dining area here is a quick, easy way to create a perfect patio layout.

Break It Up: To create privacy, don't just put up a solid wall. Make your screening more interesting and effective using varying depths, dimensions, and materials.

Fire Screen: Be sure to consider privacy when deciding where to locate a fireplace; outdoor fireplaces make an excellent screening element.

United Spaces: To ensure a harmonious plan, it's ideal to use the same designer for pool work, masonry, woodwork, and other elements. If using different professionals for different components, make sure they work together to create one integrated look.

Come Hither: Stepping stones with greenery in between are more inviting than a solid path. They offer a subtle, effective way to draw people in and encourage use of the entire yard.

Infinite Options: Using cast-in-place concrete for pool coping allows complete flexibility. Pools can be shaped to accommodate any space and colors can be custom blended to fit any scheme.

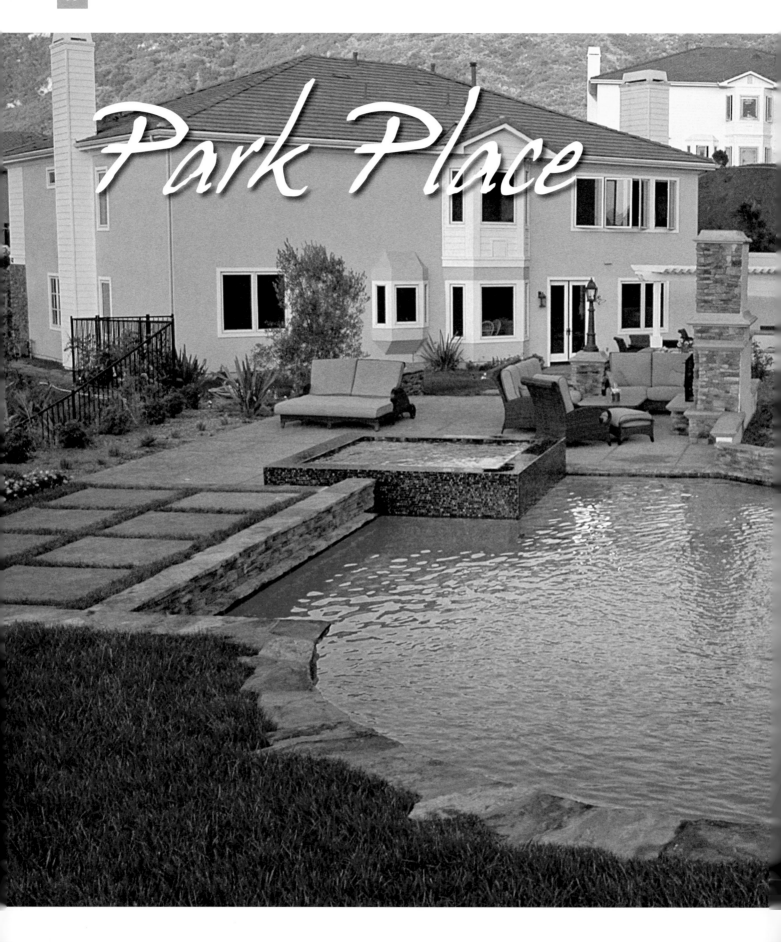

Park Place

Park Place

The view from the pool is perfect, and this coastal California backyard is all decked out for action. Guests are treated to expansive mountain vistas as they relax in the pool or sip cocktails by the fire. Sportier visitors can shoot hoops nearby.

The clients for this project wanted a pool and yard that would fit their active, athletic lifestyle and provide a beautiful setting where they could entertain guests and enjoy their spectacular surroundings. Avid dog lovers, this couple also wanted a place to swim and play with their four-legged family members. This yard was large but at an awkward angle to the house. To create this multi-purpose playground, I included a large geometric-shaped pool big enough for swimming laps, a twenty-foot slide with waterfall, and a custom-colored sport-court. When it's time to wind down, the hydrotherapy spa provides relief for active muscles. Post lamps add a decorative structural element and light the pathway. An overflow illusion spa displays a "sheet of glass" effect when not in use, capturing pristine reflections of the surrounding mountains.

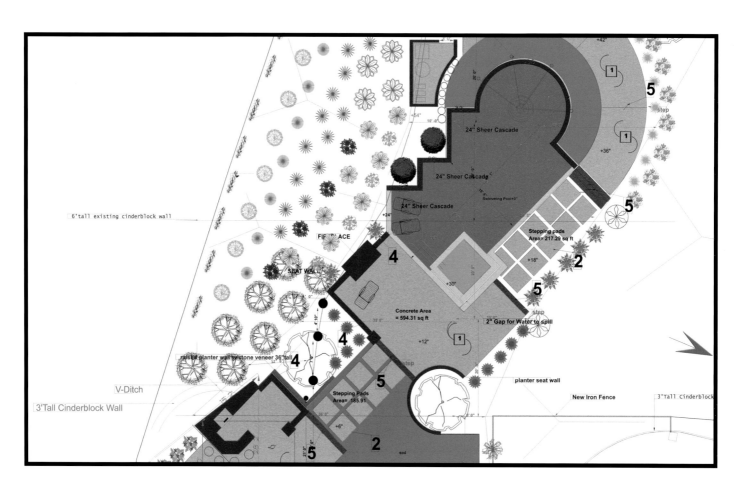

Fetch-A-Sketch.com

A series of pathways and landings take homeowners and their guests to the wider expanses of the outer yard. Stepping pads help make the transition from backyard kitchen through rose garden to outdoor living room and pool and patio beyond. Stonework repeated in the fireplace and pool helps integrate the two spaces. The unique geometric design of this pool allowed us to take full advantage of a long, irregular wedge-shaped yard.

Instead of the original massive wall out the back door, the clients now look out on the colorful tiled backsplash of their outdoor kitchen. The barbeque counter is made of cast concrete with crushed recycled glass polished to a smooth finish.

A splash of colorful tile over the fireplace adds an interesting accent and ties the living-room together with the barbeque and spa where the same tile is used in a different size. Seat walls by the fireplace define the area as a distinct room and make convenient perches. We chose vegetation that would blend into the natural California landscape and designed the plantings with wildfire-resistance in mind.

Seat walls allow guests to relax while chatting with the chef. Stamped stone-textured concrete patios coordinate well with the stonework used on the fireplace and pool walls.

The basketball court sports a spongy surface with a playful custom look. This rubberized coating is applied over a concrete slab, then custom painted.

HGTV host Brandon Johnson and Scott Cohen during filming. This project was showcased in an episode of HGTV's "*Get Out, Way Out!*"

Design Tips :

Repeat Performance: To tie elements of a large project together, repeat the use of the same materials in varying places throughout the yard. In this project, the 1"x1" tile used on the spa is used in the same color in 6"x6" on the backsplash of the barbeque and again above the mantel.

Dark Is Beautiful: Choose a darker tile color for a perimeter overflow spa. The darker the color, the greater the reflectivity.

Warming Up: Include a fire feature close to the spa so bathers can stay warm and together while one takes a break from the hot water.

Find A Way: Rather than one huge, solid patio, design several smaller patios with inviting stepping pads in between to encourage transition from one space to another.

Zones of Defense: When landscaping in a fire hazard area, plant in pockets or zones that keep flammable vegetation away from the house. Trees should be spaced 15-20 feet apart and should be kept on the periphery of the property. Keep the area within thirty feet of the house well-irrigated and planted with low growing, low-flammability species. For more information, see Firewise Communities at www.firewise.org.

Up and Down: Walls of varying heights are a great way to define outdoor rooms and add architectural interest. Use planting walls to add a punch of color at any level. Seat walls do double duty when entertaining.

Mediterranean Modern

Mediterranean Modern

Antiquity-inspired touches meet the pristine shapes of contemporary architecture in this elegant yard. The reflection of old-world columns against still glassy water makes an interesting contrast with the clean lines of the pool and spa. Throughout the yard, water pours forth its magic and fire emerges from generous troughs, like ancient offerings to the elements.

The owners of this property enjoy their hillside home and love to share it with others. They wanted ample space for entertaining in a yard that would capitalize on their amazing view. I designed a multipurpose backyard with numerous outdoor rooms that don't interrupt the horizon. The yard features an oversized perimeter-overflow spa, several lounges, and a large pool in a crisp, multifaceted design. A swim-up bar and several water and fire features offer entertainment day and night.

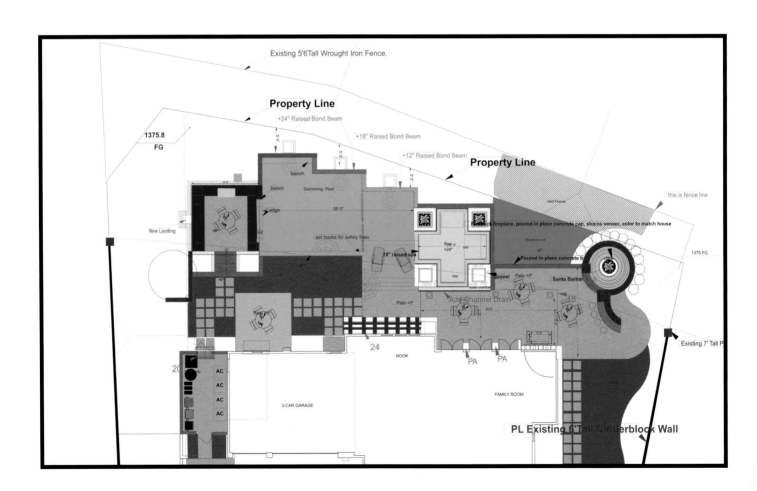

Fetch-A-Sketch.com

Large shallow scuppers with an inverse pyramid shape sit at each corner of the spa. Two hold plantings and two serve as fire bowls for night-time eye candy and warmth in the spa area. Three matching scuppers pour water into the pool.

The owners wanted a fully functioning outdoor entertainment space that wouldn't mar the view. To keep a low profile we included some below-level elements. To keep it low, we sunk the kitchen a few steps below level. We also included a "gentlemen's lounge," one of many hang-out spots in this entertaining yard.

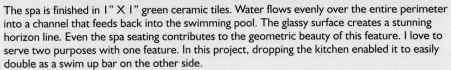

The spa is finished in 1" X 1" green ceramic tiles. Water flows evenly over the entire perimeter into a channel that feeds back into the swimming pool. The glassy surface creates a stunning horizon line. Even the spa seating contributes to the geometric beauty of this feature. I love to serve two purposes with one feature. In this project, dropping the kitchen enabled it to easily double as a swim up bar on the other side.

In a side courtyard area, water spills from two more scuppers flanking a custom stacked stone fireplace. This adds a soft "rain-stick" murmur to the crackle of the flames.

Consider the balance of weight in any design project. Here the use of oversized lumber in the pergola over the gentlemen's lounge provides shade while balancing the overall design.

The lounge shares a wall with the adjacent pool, making an ideal spot for a swim-up bar. We created another lounge on the spa-side of the pool. A circular shape, center fire pit, and plenty of cushions make this a cozy conversation area. An additional beverage bar here is a convenient serving spot for guests on this side of the yard. Stepping pads between rooms show the way without sacrificing green-space.

Design Tips :

Water Speaks: Sound is an important component of any water feature. To create the hushed rainfall quality in the fireplace water features, we inserted screens below the rim of the receiving basins. The screens break up the stream to soften the splash.

A Place for Us: When designing a yard for large gatherings include diverse hang-out spaces for different ages and social groups. In this yard the "gentlemen's lounge," conversation circle, courtyard, and pool/spa area ensures a comfortable place for everyone.

Keep it Green: Too much hardscape can be as welcoming as a parking lot on a hot day. Make sure patios and pools are wrapped with greenery to give users a cool garden experience.

Where's the Deck?: Pools are typically constructed with a five-foot concrete perimeter, but to incorporate greenery right up to the edge, pools can be engineered with a zero deck detail. Extra rebar in the bond beam bypasses the need for the additional strength of more concrete.

Material Matters: Appropriate material selection is critical for creating a cohesive design with the feel you're looking for. In this project, stone work coordinates with the colors in the scuppers, pavers, and cast concrete coping. Tumbled pavers add to the timeless, old-world feel. If we had chosen different materials, like glass tile, the look would have been completely modern.

Room With a View: Consider dropping a patio below level to keep it from blocking a view. If necessary, a submersible pump can be used to keep the area dry.

Water Meets Sky

Water Meets Sky

There's no better way to enhance a magnificent view than with a vanishing edge pool. When that pool is perched high on the side of a mountain, the effect is almost surreal.

This property offers unlimited vistas of hillsides and blue sky. With grown children and grandchildren, the owners wanted a special space where they could enjoy cocktails and sunsets with other adults and entertain younger visitors too. We gave them this vanishing edge pool with an adjacent overflow perimeter spa. An observation deck with oversized fire-bowl adds dancing flames to the ethereal display of water and sky. An outdoor kitchen/living area with a pass-through fireplace is another inviting place to catch the show.

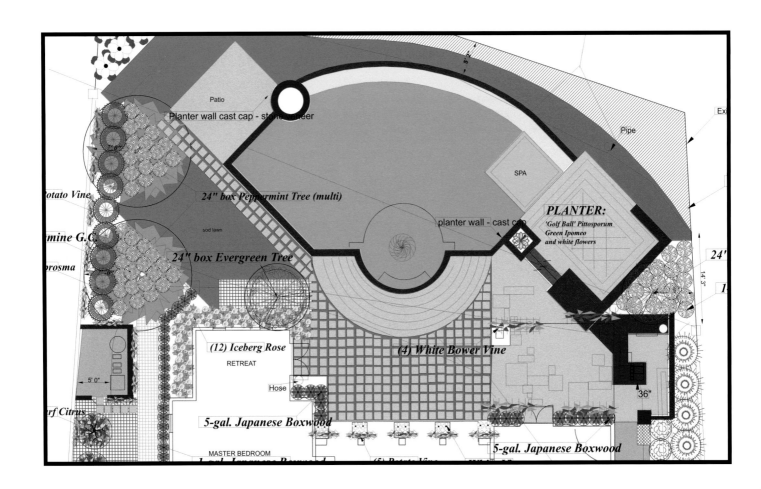

Fetch-A-Sketch.com

We designed the pool with a curved outer wall to expand the view and make the yard feel larger. Placing patios at an angle to the house also broadened this backyard. The perimeter overflow spa spills into the pool and water spills over the edge of the pool into a collection basin below. With no visible edges to support them, these sheets of water seem suspended in midair. The pop-up fountain in the Baja shelf cools off grandkids on hot days.

The kitchen's multi-tiered counter provides optimal surfaces for cooking, dining, and serving beverages.

Instead of the traditional lava rock, this fire bowl holds recycled crushed black glass chosen for its color and texture. The fire bowl's position next to the pool ensures a reflective display after dark. To add to the magic, we chose a moon garden theme for the plantings, using only white flowers and green foliage. In the light of the moon, the flowers seem to glow against their dark backdrop.

We chose a dark finish on this all-tile pool for the highest reflective quality. Its mirrored surface captures every detail of the clouds, sky, and mountains.

The pass-through fireplace divides outdoor rooms while maintaining an open view. The kitchen's multi-level counter provides optimal surfaces for cooking, dining and serving beverages.

This project earned a Gold Award for Best Swimming Pool and Spa Combination at the Western Pool and Spa Show. It was also featured on HGTV's *Get Out, Way Out!*

Design Tips :

Feeling Edgy?: Vanishing edge pools are ideally suited to properties with a high elevation or on the waterfront where they can dramatically enhance the view.

Split Level: When designing outdoor kitchen counters, include multiple levels for multiple purposes. Standard bar height is 44 inches; standard food prep height is 36 inches; standard dining height is thirty inches.

Inside Scoop: When designing the garden, consider the view from inside the house too. For this project we made sure the picture would be worthy of the home's large windows.

Fully Furnished: Don't diminish a great outdoor room with uncomfortable or undersized furniture. Take time to do it right and make sure your choices fit the style and mood you're trying to convey.

Soft Underfoot: An area rug is a quick, easy way to establish an outdoor room and give it a warm, inviting feel. Be sure to use one that's specifically designed for outdoor use. There are outdoor rugs available to fit any design scheme.

Heavy Metal: When building a fire feature close to water, use stainless steel gas rings to prolong their life.

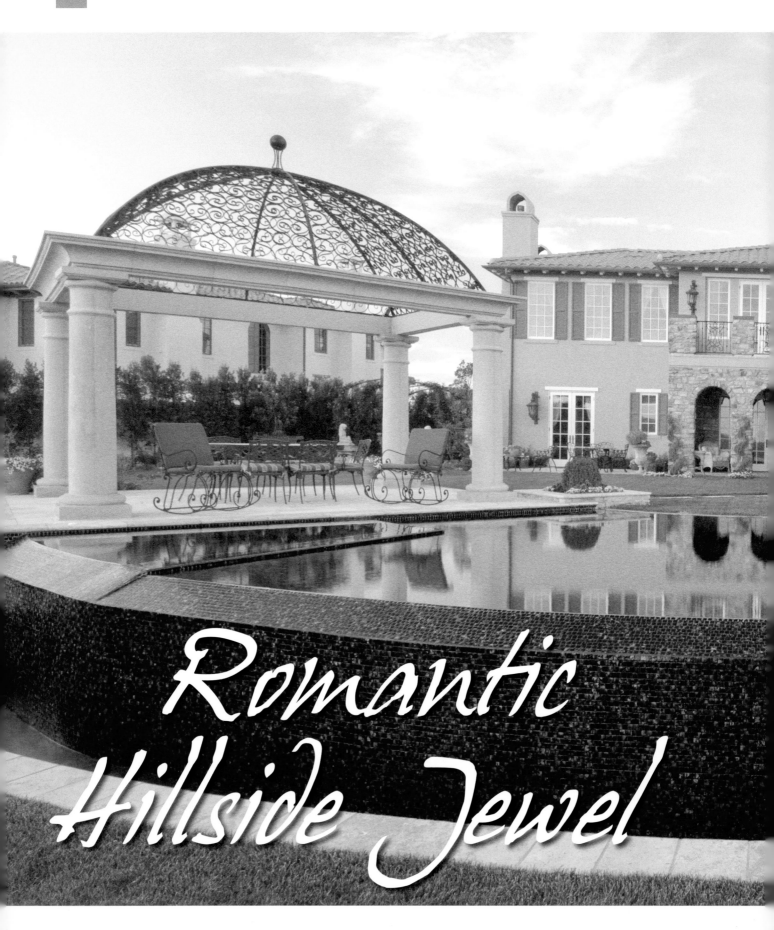

Romantic Hillside Jewel

Photo by Deidra Walpole

Romantic Hillside Jewel

The glistening surface of this sweeping, fan-shaped pool captures a pure reflection of the sky and surrounding landscape. With no visible edge on three sides, it perches on the hillside like a pristine sapphire lake. The pool was designed to capture mirror images of the home's striking architectural features.

The owners of this property are the picture of true-love. Hand-holding sweethearts, they wanted a romantic backyard where they could vacation at home while reminiscing about their favorite travels abroad.

I designed this all-tile, vanishing edge pool and spa with a fan shape to show off their view and emphasize the arches and columns of the home's beautiful Tuscan architecture. To maintain the timeless feel of that architectural style, we used rustic hardscape materials, old-world columns, and iron scrollwork in a yard that includes pool, spa, viewing deck, outdoor kitchen, and living-room.

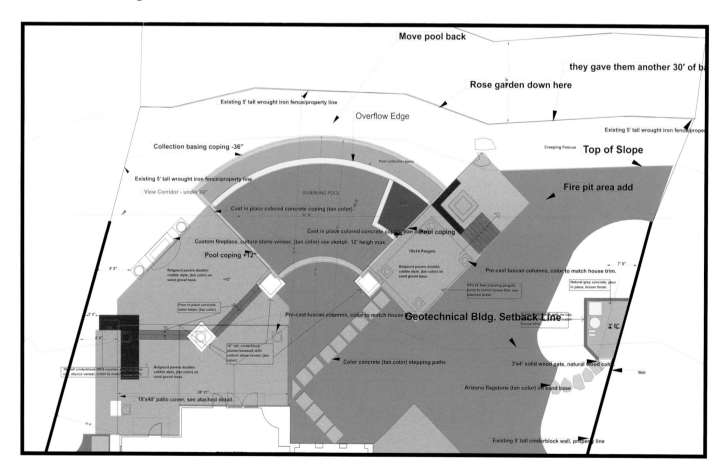

Fetch-A-Sketch.com

Photos by Deidra Walpole

The solid roof over the dining patio creates permanent shade. Flooring, pool coping, and pathways are all travertine for a timeless look and feel. A large stone fireplace anchors the living-room and provides a privacy screen from neighbors while framing the view beyond.

The kitchen counter was crafted with dark brown cast concrete embedded with crushed recycled beer bottles to give it an amber sparkle.

To achieve the glassy lake effect, both the front and back edges of the pool overflow their boundaries. The large spa is discreetly placed within the pool without interrupting the fan shape. A fire pit near the viewing deck offers another spot for warming up. Water spills into a narrow channel cut into the rear bond beam. A medallion spouts water into the collection basin, adding another authentic detail.

Photos by Deidra Walpole

The pool and spa are finished in a mosaic of 1' x 1' tiles for a shimmering, jewel-encrusted look. The oversized collection basin below the pool also serves as a fun wading pool for kids.

A dome of intricate iron scrollwork tops the columned pavilion. Sunlight passes through the columns & scrollwork, creating interesting shadow patterns & reflections throughout the day.

This yard earned a Masters of Design award from *Pool & Spa News* and was featured on HGTV's *Get Out, Way Out!* Cast and crew followed Cohen around for a year to document construction of this project.

Design Tips :

Broaden Your Horizons: Using a fan shape and a curved vanishing edge creates a more open aspect and adds a broader surface to capture the reflections of an outstanding view.

Watch For Children: A vanishing edge pool is not for everyone. The perimeter is wet and slippery and may not be the safest choice for small children who like to play on the edges.

Drop Off!: With an all-tile veneer, it can be difficult to tell how deep the pool is. This illusion adds to the beauty but can be surprising too.

Don't Get Soaked: Be sure to waterproof both the inside and outside walls in a vanishing edge pool.

Fireplace or Fire pit?: Fireplaces and fire pits establish two distinct moods. A fireplace encourages people to pull up a chair close to the hearth for quiet relaxation. A fire pit, on the other hand, keeps the conversation flowing as the group gathers in a circle facing one another to share stories and jokes.

Instant Mosaic: To achieve the mosaic effect, select a tile with variations in shade between individual pieces.

Heaven Scent: Aromatherapy is a delightful way to set the right mood. Spark romance with fragrant plantings.

Libation Sensations

Libation Sensations

Color and light. Water and flame. This yard, which offers plenty of amusement by day, turns on its real magic at night.

With young children, these clients wanted a yard to accentuate their gorgeous golf course view without the safety issues of a vanishing edge pool. They also wanted a pool large enough for lap swims. As wine connoisseurs, they wanted a unique, entertaining nightspot where they could enjoy libations with friends.

We showcased the view from this Mediterranean-themed yard with a slot-overflow spa framed by two large fire bowls. To allow for a 50 foot swim line, the pool extends under a balustrade bridge which leads to the raised outdoor living room. We added an outdoor hot spot worthy of Dionysius himself with a recycled wine bottle counter accented with fascinating light and color effects.

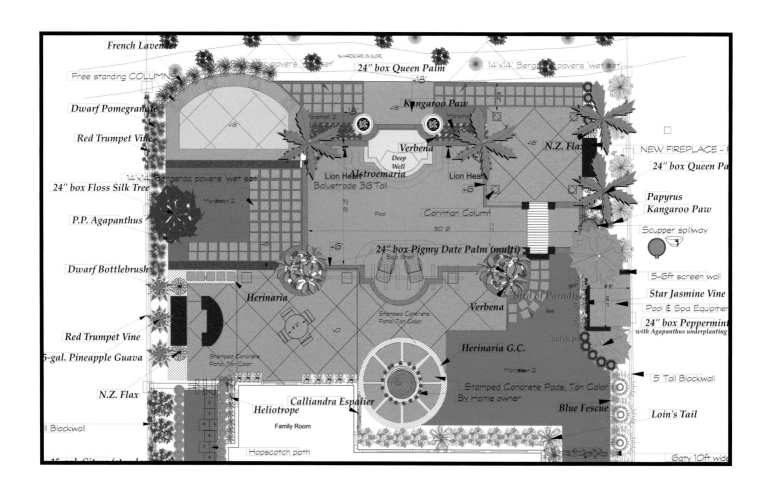

Fetch-A-Sketch.com

We embedded the countertop with pieces of recycled colored glass and actual wine and scotch bottles that I melted in my kiln. The counter is lit from below using 500 fiber-optic cables. The after-hours effect is dazzling.

The pool interior is finished with a blend of blue and green 3M Colorquartz Crystals.

We situated the spa on the same level as the raised patios. As water spills down the steps it is collected in a quarter-inch slot and is then re-circulated in the pool. A veil of water cascades down the steps of the spa accented with two lion-head medallion wall fountains. An extra-large Baja shelf allows several guests to take in the view from the pool together.

The slot overflow spa creates an effect similar to that of a vanishing edge pool but without the safety issue.

When the sun goes down, the show continues as reflections of flames dance on water. We used bull-nose travertine coping and tumbled concrete pavers to enhance the old-world ambiance.

HGTV's *Property Buzz* filming

We created the base of the barbeque counter using 250 recycled wine bottles collected by the owners during wine-tasting excursions.

Design Tips :

Light Effects: Night lighting is a major component of a quality backyard design. Think about safety first by lighting your walkways. Light focal points using up-lighting techniques. Use down-lighting to accent columns or dining areas. Show interesting surface textures with a "grazing" effect that spreads a wash of light to bring out fine shadows.

Vanishing Act: There are different ways to achieve the aesthetic of a rimless pool or spa. A designer familiar with the latest pool construction and engineering techniques can discuss your options.

Arms Length: Adding a bridge is a great way to lengthen a pool without sacrificing needed yard space. Make sure the bridge is raised enough to allow swimmers a full reach underneath.

Optical Allure: If considering a vanishing edge design, make sure it will accentuate a view you love. There's no point using it to highlight your neighbor's fence.

Positively Illuminating: A pool finished in a lighter blue-green color gives off a sexy, almost phosphorescent glow when lit at night.

Gimme Shelter: Pergolas add shade and the feeling of shelter without completely blocking the sun. They also provide a structure for climbing plants.

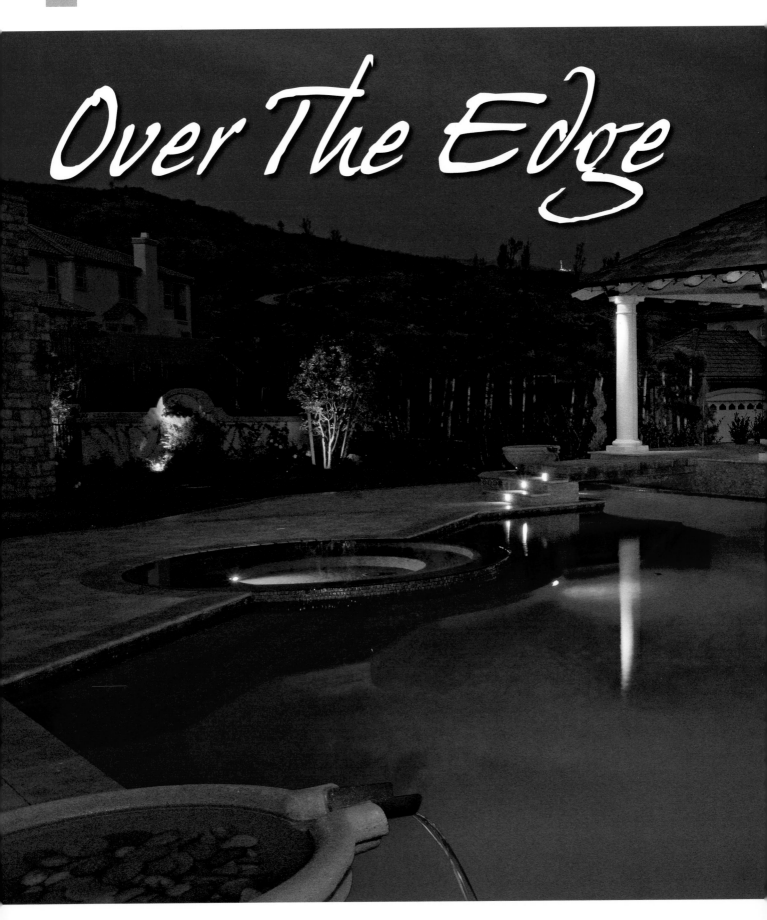

Over The Edge

Over the Edge

Overlooking the hills of California's San Fernando Valley, this striking poolscape seems to take swimmers to infinity … *and beyond*. It's a great example of the illusion created when water seems to go just a bit too far.

The owner wanted to make a bold statement in a backyard with Mediterranean style and plenty of "wow!" The property enjoys a romantic valley view, so it was important to create just the right frame for this sweeping landscape.

The property was a natural for a vanishing edge pool. We framed this one with two massive fire bowls, creating a substantial anchor on each side of the waterline. A round perimeter overflow spa on the opposite side sits nearly level with the water, giving bathers a perfect vantage point for appreciating this trompe l'oeil.

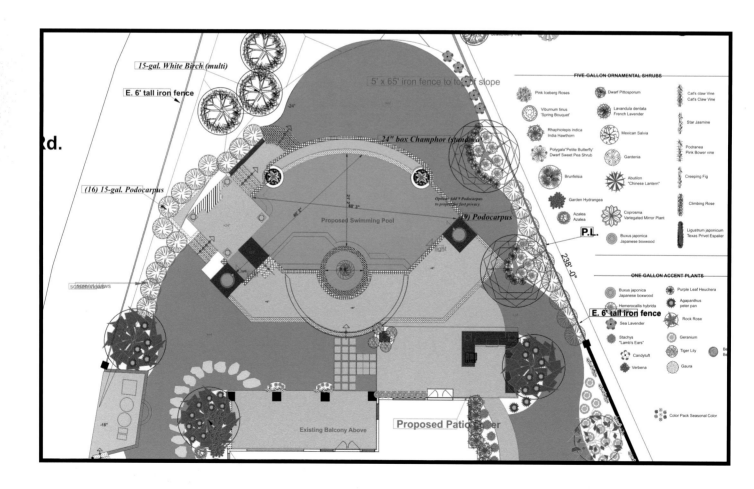

Fetch-A-Sketch.com

A bridge crosses the pool to an outdoor living-room with a large wood-burning fireplace as its focal point.

Photos by Paul Jonason

The circular spa, almost level with the water, doesn't interrupt the wide-open expanse of the pool. Water from the all-tile spa spills into a narrow channel that flows back into the swimming pool.

On opposite sides of the pool, gentle streams of water pour from two generous cast concrete scuppers that coordinate with the fire-bowls. These water features add sound and visual interest without disturbing the reflective quality of the pool. The scuppers perch on slightly elevated platforms, and are beautifully reflected in the pool's mirror surface.

Photos by Paul Jonason

The barbeque counter is constructed of cast concrete with crushed recycled glass. It is polished with several finishing tools to a lustrous finish. The two-level counter offers the optimum height for both cooking and serving. A decorative stone mosaic provides a Mediterranean accent between the two levels. Classically styled decorative corbels on the side of the barbeque seem to support the countertop.

Design Tips :

Do Not Disturb: Be careful adding a water feature to a vanishing edge pool. Make sure it won't disturb the reflective quality you're after.

No Wake: In infinity pools, always use a diverter on returns in the floor so you don't see water movement on the surface.

Smooth Circulation: Use a skimmer at the upper level for leaf collection along with two pumps: one for circulating the upper pool and one for circulating the overflow edge. New energy efficient variable speed pumps allow you to set the pump at the lowest speed and still get water movement.

Get Edge-iocated: The more precisely level your edge detail, the less water you'll need to move in order to achieve the effect and the less energy you'll use.

Traffic Control: When designing a yard for entertaining, keep pathways and bridges wider than three feet to allow for two-way traffic.

A Burning Issue: A hot cocktail dress is one thing; but if it's actually on fire, it's not pretty. Keep fire features out of main traffic areas and consider prevailing wind directions when choosing a location.

Fire and Water

Fire and Water

Like a modern temple honoring the primal forces of nature, this melding of fire and water speaks to the soul. Pure, clean, controlled lines contrast against the wild abandon of leaping flames.

This yard needed a modern makeover to match the artistic, contemporary look of the client's renovated home. The owner wanted a pool and spa plus outdoor rooms for entertaining. However, an upslope in the side yard presented space challenges.

By making use of different levels, we carved out room for a sizable pool, a deep-well spa, and ample space for hosting company. We included a fascinating combination of fire and water features throughout the yard for a study in contrasts that embodies energies of yin and yang. This yard earned a gold award for Best Water Feature Design at the 2008 Western Pool and Spa Show.

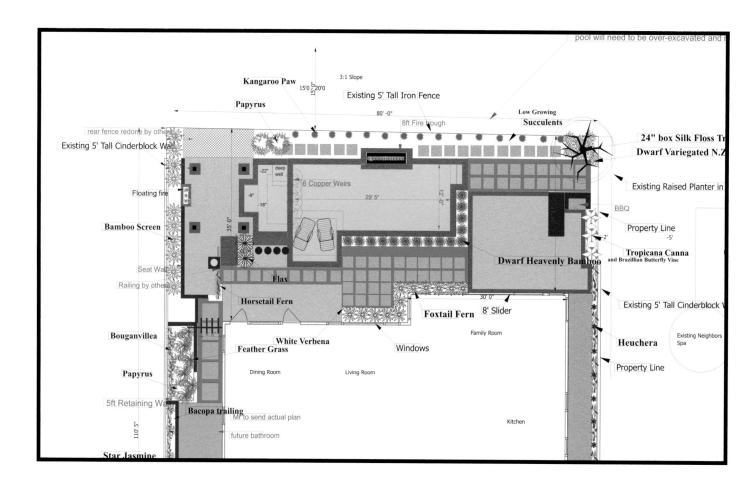

Fetch-A-Sketch.com

Heated water pours from the overhead shelter for a pounding over-the-shoulder massage. In contrast, a sheer ripple of water descends from spa to pool with gentle softness. The pool, spa, and "floating fire" feature are finished with sparkling glass tile.

A fire trough lines one side of the pool. Beyond the curtain of water over the spa, a small basin of fire seems to hover midair. The fire feature behind the spa includes a fill-and-spill feature. Water fills the collecting basin then spills over the glass tile for a continuously changing sheen.

In the countertop, oversize chunks of blue and clear glass are lit from below with fiber-optics for dazzling cocktail-hour entertainment.

Coping was white cast concrete. Stepping pads in between are pre-cast white concrete. These allow us to introduce more greenery into the yard while still maintaining walking space for two-way traffic. Fiber optic lights embedded in the pool floor create a grazing effect to show off the texture of the cast concrete ripple wall across the front of the spa.

Raising the deep-well spa three feet allowed us to make full use of the side yard and create space for an additional outdoor room.

An outdoor kitchen sits opposite the spa. Its base of contemporary glass block is lit with fiber optic cables woven between each course. With the help of a color wheel, the glass glows with subtle, changing hues.

The cast concrete ripple wall is stained with acid chemicals to coordinate with the tile. The forceful rush of the waterfall combined with the gentle rain-stick sound of the ripple wall is intoxicating.

Design Tips :

Clean and Pure: A simple plant palette of grasses and low-mounding plants works well for a contemporary landscape design.

Spread the Fire: When creating a fire trough, loop gas plumbing for even flames across the entire feature.

Look Out Below: When lighting a stairway, use either embedded step lights or side lights. Never light stairs from above; this creates shadows that make it difficult to spot the next step.

Details Details: When designing around any theme, the smallest details matter. In this project, the custom-fabricated stainless steel handrail on the patio steps adds an appropriate detail for a contemporary design.

Double Take: Look for ways to make features work overtime. The overhanging edge of this spa doubles as a functional bar counter, making another great space for guests in and out of the water to mingle.

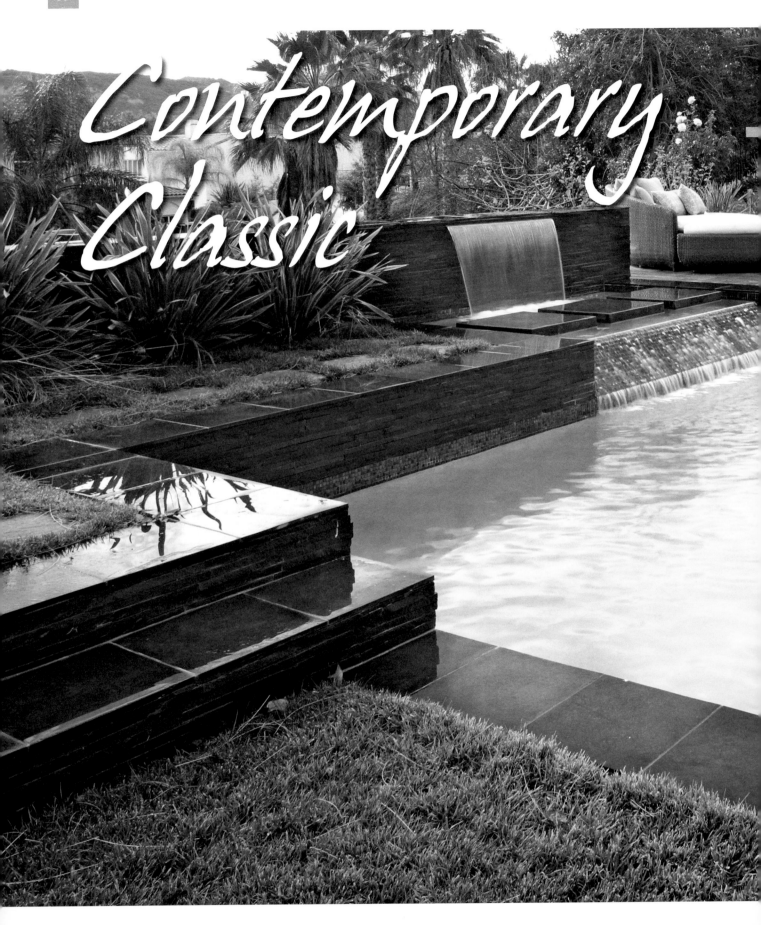

Contemporary Classic

Photo by Paul Jonason

Contemporary Classic

This pool/spa makeover took a yard with a '70's version of "modern" and transformed it into a contemporary composition for today. Now this geometric landscape sports all the right angles.

After gutting and remodeling the interior of his home, the owner needed a backyard renovation to match. The inside reflected the owner's appreciation for pure lines and exquisite materials. He wanted his outdoor spaces to do the same.

Together we designed a series of outdoor rooms made to entertain including pool, spa, barbeque, and living area accented with interesting fire and water features. A unique waterfall takes center stage. Three large, square, polished concrete stepping pads "float" between two cascades, offering an extraordinary walk-on-water experience.

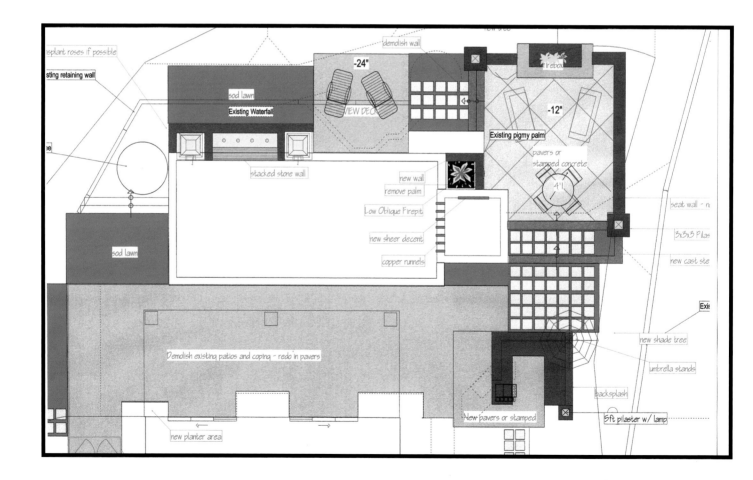

Fetch-A-Sketch.com

Photos by Paul Jonason

The right amount of color and curve make this contemporary backyard super comfy too. The orange fireplace and seat cushions add a bold punch of fiery color in the outdoor living area. A massive square fire bowl on one side of the waterfall resonates with the planter on the opposite side. The living-room fountain repeats the stacked slate used in the pool waterfall. The cantilevered concrete mantle pops against the color-saturated fireplace.

We took the existing shell of a pool and recreated it to fit the homeowner's taste for modern architecture and distinctive—even rare—materials. Rectangles, squares, long lines, and cool colors gave this yard the precise geometric vibe we were after.

We extended the coping lines from the pool and spa to create step lines and a raised area for the outdoor living room. In this project, the owner's dedication to finding just the right materials paid off. Dark slate, iridescent black glass tiles, stainless steel, and soft gray concrete unite to create the perfect feel. Water flowing over the lower cascade shimmers against the iridescent black tile.

Photos by Paul Jonason

Several custom-fabricated stainless steel weirs in the spa, pool, and outdoor living room match the stainless steel cascades in the walk-across water feature.

The pool is finished underwater with a blend of blue and black 3M Colorquartz Crystals. The combination of slate coping and 1" x 1" black glass tile in the pool area makes a striking accent that continues throughout.

The kitchen backsplash and an inset in the counter walls feature an unusual stainless steel tile that forms a rich contrast against the stacked stone walls and polished concrete countertop.

Sometimes a water feature is so inviting, you just have to be a part of it. This walk-on-waterfall offers just that opportunity.

Design Tips :

Find a Seat: Design fountain walls at seat height to create additional space for guests.

Show Some Restraint: Use stone as you would makeup on a pretty face. Don't layer it on thick. Instead, save it to highlight special features.

Have Shade, Will Travel: Built in umbrella stands in all counters allow you to move umbrellas around to follow the sun.

Echo, Echo: Even in seemingly minor details, repetition of simple shapes can add harmony to a design. Here the pyramid shape of the light fixtures is echoed and inverted in the planter and fire bowl.

Geometry At Play

Photo by Deidra Walpole

Geometry at Play

A pair of playful hippos cavorts on the lawn, throwing a humorous curve into the lines and angles of this geometric showplace. The hippos say it all: This yard was made to amuse.

The casual, fun-loving owners of this property find a lot of joy in entertaining. Large parties are their specialty, so they needed plenty of space for guests to spread out, kick back, and have a good time.

We gave them a full suite of outdoor rooms in a resort-like yard that includes an oversized pool, a hydrotherapy spa, an outdoor kitchen, and a cozy living room accessible by a short walk across the water. The modern, open design is all squares and rectangles surrounding an expanse of lush green lawn.

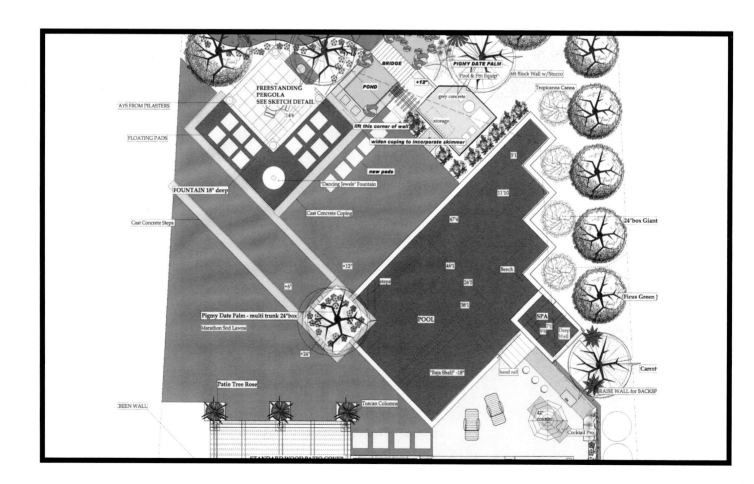

Photos by Nick Lucero and
Deidra Walpole

Fetch-A-Sketch.com

The large stepping stones to the living room seem to float on the water but are actually supported from below on concrete columns. The Tuscan feel of the fireplace and living room match the style of the new-construction home. The pool walls are veneered with faux stone. The same treatment is applied to the walls of the counter and the living room pilasters. Pool coping is cast concrete in a coordinating color.

The bar counter, made of cast concrete embedded with recycled glass, is lit from below with fiber optics.

Multiple water features add to the festivities. Near the living room, water pours from pilaster medallions and a fountain mixes things up a bit. In the pool, water cascades from stainless steel weirs and a matching weir in the spa provides a heated water massage. "The oversized pool features a generous Baja shelf that can hold a small group of loungers."

Photos by Nick Lucero and Deidra Walpole

To make way for this suite of rooms while maintaining an open feel, we took advantage of every part of the yard. The unique geometric pool design makes full use of available space. The elevated spa combines well with the outdoor kitchen and bar.

A lion head medallion shower offers a quick après-swim rinse. Carefully placed gargoyles watch over the scene, keeping spirits high.

Raising the spa to bar height allowed a perfect place to tie in a swim up bar and outdoor kitchen. Whether wet or dry, guests can relax on either side of the bar.

This property was featured on HGTV's "Big Splash," a special presentation featuring the ultimate in pool design from around the country.

Design Tips :

Channel Your Inner Designer: Be sure to explore different design concepts before making final decisions. These clients originally wanted a more Mediterranean theme. After I showed them different options, we chose a concept with a completely different feel.

Night Magic: A combination of different lighting effects creates a mesmerizing nighttime display. Here the counter is lit from below with fiber-optics. Throughout the yard, trees are accented with uplighting. Under-surface lights illuminate the fountains for a "shower-of-diamonds" effect.

Your Go-to Spot: To encourage use of the entire yard, create a distant "go-to" focal point. We purposely placed the living-room across the yard to provide an inviting destination for guests.

Find Your Level: Use bands, steps, and plantings to create different levels. Here bands of lawn stretch across the yard to create different plateaus and an expansive resort-like feel.

Control The Action: Create separate valves for each water feature. This way you can turn up a pool fountain without having the nearby wall fountain shooting all the way across the lawn. (We learned the hard way.)

Artist At Work: If you've found a great designer, allow him or her some artistic license. Sometimes, what you think you want might not quite suit your home. A good designer will listen to your needs and give you what you're really looking for in a landscape that fits your property.

Flipped Out

Photo by Deidra Walpole

Flipped Out

What happens when you take a vanishing edge pool and turn it around? You get a stunning, dive-in water feature that's gorgeous no matter how you look at it.

With boundless valley views, this hillside property called out for a vanishing edge pool. But the typical design, with the rimless side overlooking the hill, would have entailed exorbitant construction costs in this small, steeply sloped yard.

So we flipped the design around. With the vanishing side now facing the house, the view is set off by glistening sheets of water as they flow over the precise lines, angles, and bevels of this elegantly shaped pool. The unique geometric design of the pool made full use of available space and allowed us to incorporate a 45-foot swimline (the length of a straight stretch in the pool used for swimming laps). To fulfill the rest of the big wish list for this small yard we added a spa, outdoor kitchen, and fire pit along with living room and dining patios.

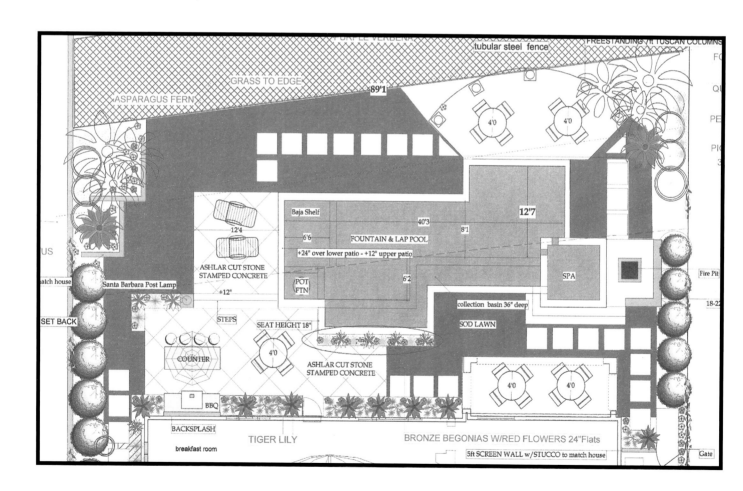

Fetch-A-Sketch.com

Photos by
Deidra Walpole

The spa repeats the strong square profile of the basin beneath the urn fountain. The geometry of the spa continues in the adjacent fire pit. The spa wall plays a dual role by offering seating next to the fire. Another seat wall completes the square around the fire pit. The bias-laid ceramic tile on the overflow edge was a tricky installation, but resulted in a beautiful way to show off the refined angles of the pool.

Living room and dining patios offer optimal spots for viewing the hillsides and pool. The illusion of water flowing toward the house generates feelings of positive energy and well-being.

By flipping this design, we solved the construction challenges caused by tricky site conditions without sacrificing the reflectivity of a vanishing edge pool. Water bubbles from an oversized urn fountain and spills from custom copper weirs into the pool. From there, it slips over a sleek beveled edge into a collection basin below. The urn fountain is cast concrete in a rich adobe color.

Photos by Deidra Walpole

The stepping pads from the kitchen to the dining area to the viewing deck and spa area demonstrate thoughtful use of "wayfinding." The paths draw people into the next space and encourage use of the entire yard.

The counter and bar surfaces are constructed of lightly polished adobe concrete. The backsplash and pool areas are finished with a variegated ceramic tile in brown tones.

Color is an important unifying element in this design. The warm browns, rusts, and tans of the Three Rivers flagstone used in the fountain, spa, and fire pit provide the foundation for the color scheme.

The bottom of the pool is finished with blue and black 3M Colorquartz Crystals for full reflectivity.

Design Tips :

Take It To the Limit: Using a zero deck detail allows you to bring greenery right up to the pool edge.

Mix It Up: Don't be afraid to use a variety of hardscape materials in your outdoor rooms. This design uses a combination of genuine stone, faux stone, cast concrete, and ceramic tile. The key is to bring it all together with coordinating colors.

Step It Up: Remember to include vertical interest in your design. Each new step adds a new level of interest. In this design, it wasn't structurally necessary to include the tiled curbing around the overflow collection basin. But the curbing added tremendously to the geometric lines of the yard.

Be Size Wise: When working in a small yard, pay careful attention to space in your patios. How many people will you accommodate in each room? How will the furniture fit? Here, making some patios small and intimate, allowed for a generous layout in others.

Minor Matters: Find ways to continue your design in even the smallest details. Step risers may seem like an insignificant component of the landscape, but here they become a beautiful piece of the picture when finished with old-world vintage tiles.

Grow Your Yard: Using greenery between stepping stones expands the feel of a smaller yard.

Good Reflections

Good Reflections

Searching for inner bliss? An Asian-inspired pool like this might help you find it.

The young professional couple who owned this property wanted a yard to help them find tranquility after hectic days at work. With a baby on the way, they needed a pool that worked for young children too.

We gave them a landscape that's soothing in its simplicity. With pure lines and a quiet palette, the yard exudes a calming, less-is-more attitude. The glassy water of the overflow spa invites reflection. The Baja shelf, with a narrow opening that's easy to cordon off, makes a stress-free wading pool for young children. We also found room in this small yard for an outdoor kitchen and fire pit, making it an ideal place to chill out and enjoy this home's magnificent sunsets. The addition of after-hours color in the spa puts the finishing touch on a relaxing evening.

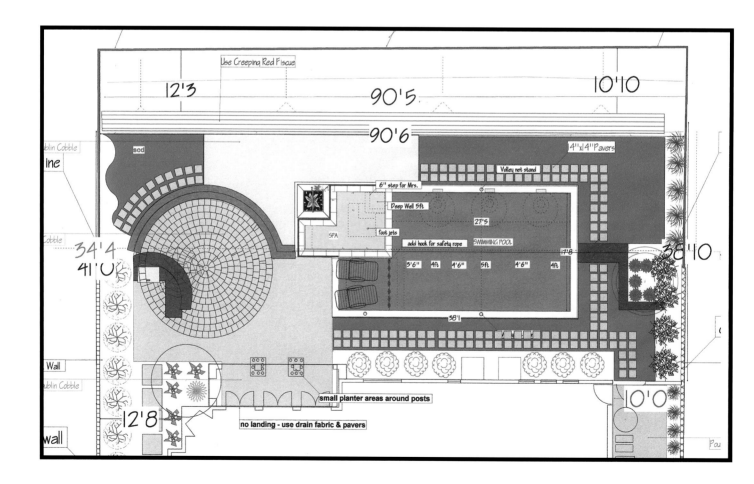

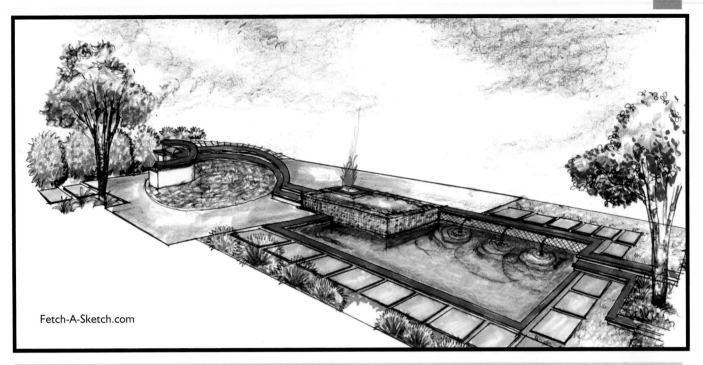

Fetch-A-Sketch.com

Making room for a pool, spa, kitchen, and fire pit in this small yard was a challenge. A clean, modern design fit the space and created the meditative feel the clients were looking for. Water in the perimeter overflow spa pours into a slotted copper channel. In certain lights, the undisturbed surface gives the spa the appearance of a precisely cut block of pure glass. The pool wall is finished with El Dorado faux stone to coordinate with the kitchen counter. Coping is cast concrete.

The kitchen area packs a lot into a compact footprint, reserving ample space in the adjacent patio for seating around the fire and spa. The counter is designed with split levels and a curved profile that offers plenty of cooking/serving area at arm's reach.

Square cast concrete pavers with grass in between lead to each area of the yard without sacrificing too much lawn.

The sides of the counter are veneered in El Dorado faux stone. The countertop is adobe-colored cast concrete with a medium polish.

The square fire pit is set directly at level with the spa and completes the spa's clean rectangle shape. Water spills around the entire perimeter of the spa, creating a reflective sheen right up to the edge of the fire pit. The patio is laid with tumbled concrete pavers with a circle medallion in the center.

Underwater lighting changes subtly with sixteen different color patterns.

The spa is finished in a mosaic of 1"x1" imported Japanese tiles from Fujiwa in varying shades of celadon and jade with cobalt blue accents.

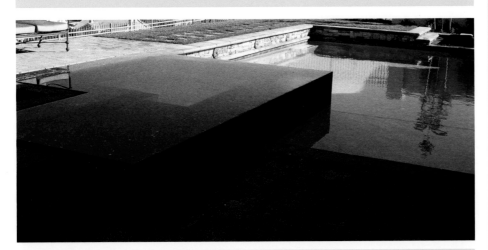

Raising the spa slightly and including a stepped-up level added vertical interest to the pool and yard.

Design Tips :

Serenity Now: To create a restful retreat, keep lines and shapes simple, use low-key furnishings, and make sure water and fire features don't overwhelm the space.

Simply Beautiful: A low-profile fire pit is more discreet and consistent with a minimalist design than a large fireplace. Plus it won't spoil the view.

Just Passing Though: Even in a small yard, make sure to include ample width in pathways. A yard will feel even smaller if two people can't pass each other comfortably on a path.

Waves Of Color: Changing pool and spa lights add both color and motion to the landscape. The mesmerizing display offers subtle entertainment after dark.

Sinking Deep: A deep-well spa offers the ultimate in full-body relaxation. It's a must-have for any poolscape that emphasizes reflection and rejuvenation.

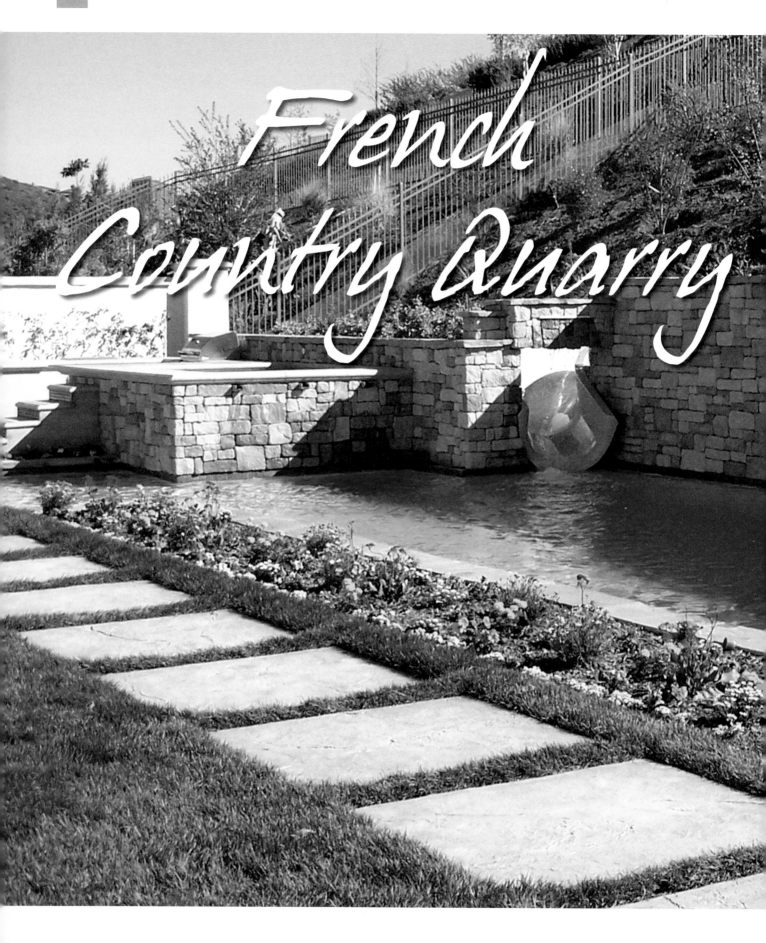

French
Country Quarry

French Country Quarry

This sunny hillside pool has the look and feel of a peaceful rock quarry somewhere in the south of France. But the quiet is frequently broken with laughter, as one child after another races down the giant slide and tumbles into the water.

This client has kids in all age groups and wanted a yard to maximize amusement for them, their friends, and adults too. A spa where teens could entertain friends and a pool that offered plenty of opportunity for sliding and jumping in were both high on the wish list.

An upslope posed a challenge, but we decided to capitalize on this by creating a pool with high stone walls that also serve as a retaining system. We added a commercial grade 52-foot fiberglass slide that gives swimmers young and old a wild ride.

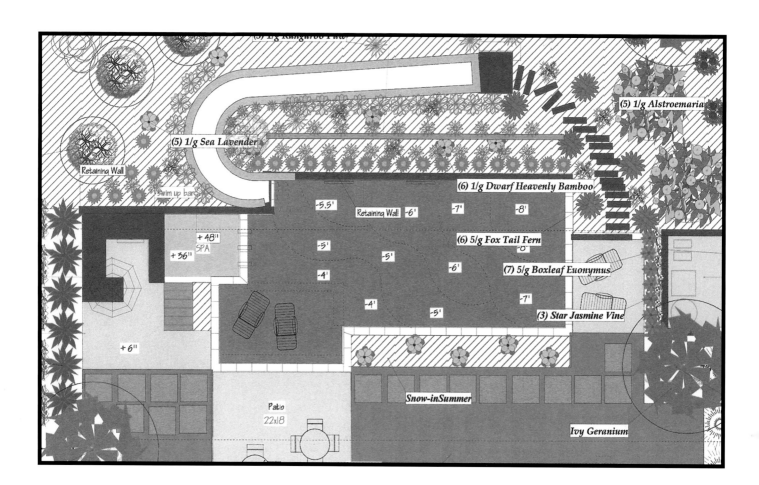

Fetch-A-Sketch.com

With a sizeable outdoor kitchen, comfortable outdoor living areas, colorful flowers, and soothing water features, there's something for everyone in this French country poolscape. The spa, which comfortably accommodates six to eight people, makes a great hangout for teens or adults. Three spouts arc from spa to pool. Each water feature is on a separate pump for individualized control of each. Built-in umbrella stands provide shade around the counter and spa.

This yard was a natural for a long and thrilling water slide. We created this fiberglass flume with the help of SlideScapes, a company that specializes in commercial grade slides for the residential market.

With four sides, the outdoor kitchen counter wraps almost completely around the cook. This puts a generous amount of counter space within arms reach. Raising the spa to counter height and placing it next to the kitchen allow the spa and kitchen to share a counter for swim-up bar service. A seating ledge below the water line offers a place to rest against the wall underneath the falling water.

The challenging upslope actually helped create some of this yard's best features. The stepped stone walls add architectural beauty. They also happen to be just perfect for climbing up and jumping off into the water. By screening the area with careful plantings, we gave this family all the action of a genuine water park slide without the commercial fiberglass look. The two-tiered retaining wall allows plantings at various levels, which softens the entire length of slide.

Three large cascades send sheets of water off the back wall. A cascade above the water-slide exit gives a final splash on this water park style ride.

The stamped, colored concrete used in the patios and stepping pads coordinates well with the look of natural stone.

This yard was featured on HGTV's *Get Out, Way Out!*
Scott Cohen discusses the project with host, Brandon Johnson.

Design Tips :

Waterpark Wow: Lightweight fiberglass slides reduce engineering costs and are now becoming available to the residential market. They come in all sizes and, with modular components, they can be readily customized to any landscape.

This Is Living: To bring that genuine living room feeling outdoors, start with outdoor carpets to define the space. Add comfortable, deep-seating furniture like these pieces from Patio World. Arrange conversational clusters around a table or fire.

Rest Easy: A pool with a raised wall can function as a beautiful retaining wall. But be sure to include hand holds and/or a bench along any high wall to give swimmers a safe resting spot. This pool includes a bench several inches below the water line where even young swimmers can sit with their head above water.

Slide Smart: Be sure to seek professional expertise in your slide design. (We had to add an extra curve in this one to slow things down a bit.) With the help of companies like SlideScapes, you can create an exciting and safe waterpark experience.

Maintain The Zip: Waxing your slide once or twice annually with a high-grade paste wax will help it last forever and keep the rides speedy.

Roman Pleasure Garden

Roman Pleasure Garden

This classically inspired landscape is all about style, opulence, and old-world luxury. With Italianesque details and elegant water features, the yard is designed for long, lazy afternoons and sophisticated evening entertainment.

The clients for this landscape weren't a couple but a brother/sister pair who owned the home jointly. Despite typical sibling flare-ups, there was one thing they could always agree on: they both wanted a showcase yard where they could throw parties in high style.

We created this Roman style pleasure-garden with details borrowed from sumptuous Italian estates. Columns, fountains, oversized urns, and detailed ornamentation all reflect a lavish style that will never go out of fashion.

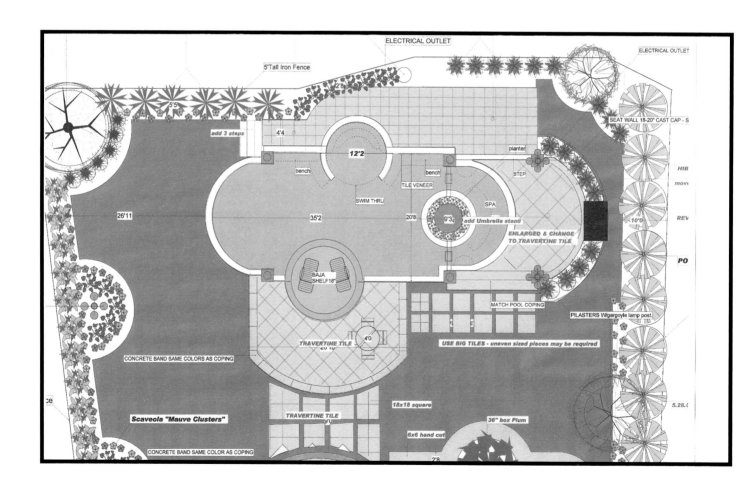

Fetch-A-Sketch.com

It took creative engineering and a collaboration of talents to create this dome-topped water feature. The water feature mechanism, a 10' long curved Sheer Descent waterfall from Polaris, had to rest above the pergola without bearing the weight of the dome. With a structural engineer, we designed posts with C-shaped brackets to discreetly float the dome over the columns. Steel poles extending through the columns and four feet below the bottom of the pool, support the mass.

Roman inspired columns support a circular gazebo topped with a custom iron-work dome. A curtain of water rains from the dome, forming a sheltered "room" within the pool. Together, the sound and mist create a unique sensory experience. A pop up fountain in the Baja shelf adds another entertaining water feature.

I coaxed a boat-builder friend, Steve Phillips, out of retirement to build a circular, waterproof structure to encase the water feature unit. This donut-shaped structure protects the water feature while supporting the hefty dome. The sound of the cascading rain shower echoes within the circular gazebo, which features seat benches around its perimeter. Twenty copper misters are plumbed into the room.

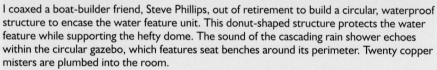

The kitchen/dining area is veneered with authentic stacked stone. Roman style arches frame the view for cook and diners. The cast concrete counters allowed us to insert posts through the surface to continue the circle of columns. Cast concrete pavers in a coordinating color form a path between outdoor rooms.

The living room deck is anchored by an old world brick wood-burning fireplace. Both living room patio and kitchen/dining patio are finished with travertine tile.

Fountains are core to the Italian pleasure-garden theme. The spa wraps around an elaborate fountain in a U shape that offers a good view from any seat.

The outdoor kitchen/dining area is cooled with twenty-five copper misters embedded in the balcony.

Design Tips :

Repeat Performance: Repeating basic shapes helps tie a landscape together. The circles and arches in this yard make it clear that each separate area is part of one cohesive plan.

Traffic Update: You can use thoughtfully placed posts and pillars to help manage traffic flow. Here the columns in the kitchen area frame the view while they slow down pedestrians (and running children) near the barbeque.

Forever Spring: Part of the cool, refreshing effect of this backyard is created by including as much green lawn and foliage as possible around the hardscape. No matter how small the yard, keep part of it green for a fresh, expansive feel.

Water View: When adding water features, keep the design of your seating and patio areas in mind. It's nice to be able to sit with friends and enjoy the view. This yard includes seating with a prime view around every water feature.

Dial It Up Or Down: Put water features on separate valves so you can dial them up, down or off depending on your mood.

Screen Scene: Locate trees and shrubs judiciously to create shelter and "walls" where needed. This yard uses trees and the fireplace on one side to screen the neighboring yard but uses low-growing shrubs on the other to maintain the hillside view.

Photo by Paul Jonason

Five Star Fabulous

This sprawling poolscape blurs the line between indoors and out, creating a garden worthy of the courtyard in an old world Spanish palace.

When the owners of this property took a vacation in Toledo, Spain, they fell in love with the city, the architecture, and the Spanish way of life. They wanted a pool to remind them of their trip and a yard to match their Mediterranean style home. With a very active social life, they also wanted a place to throw memorable parties.

We didn't leave anything out of this backyard resort. With multiple water and fire features, an indoor/outdoor pool with swim-up bar and an oversized all-tile spa, there's something here to delight all the senses. The luxurious setting is an entertainer's dream with two outdoor kitchens, two big-screen TV's, a bathroom/changing room, and even a dance floor.

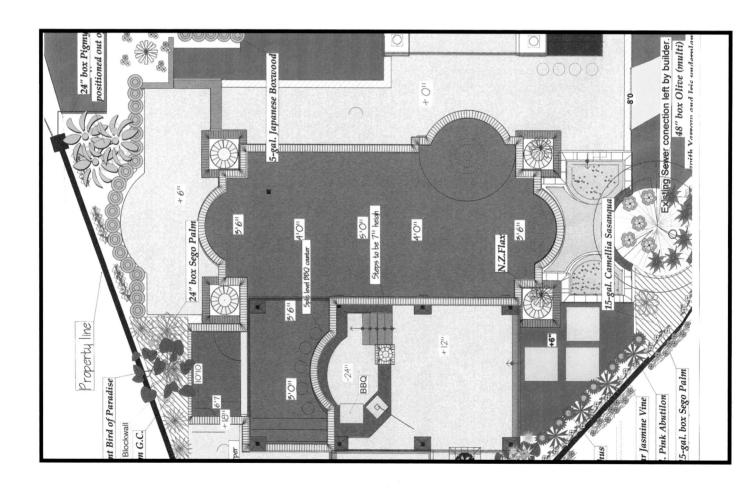

Fetch-A-Sketch.com

The deep well spa invites a purifying, relaxing soak. Finished in a mosaic of 1" X 1" sapphire blue ceramic tiles, it features a perimeter overflow detail. By day it captures reflections of the sky and architecture; at night it catches light from the surrounding fire bowls and chandeliers. Because the pillars emerge from the base of the pool, they required some extra structural engineering. Extra engineering also enabled us to design them with a more substantial profile.

Tongue and groove construction, rustic beams, and hand-forged wrought iron chandeliers add to the pavilion's old-world ambiance. Four spillways pour water from the pavilion columns. Each is outfitted with fiber optic cables that light the flowing water as it emerges.

A series of pillars and arches support the roof of a Spanish style pavilion. This large, open-air room houses a dining area, a living room, a bar, and a sunken outdoor kitchen. It also shades a section of the pool. The generous swim-up counter is designed with a curved sushi bar style configuration. Five built-in stools are finished in 1" X 1" tiles that match the spa.

Photos by Paul Jonason and Nick Lucero

The L-shaped pool and adjoining spa offer a refreshing series of indoor and outdoor "rooms." After soaking up some sun, swimmers can paddle indoors under the shade and sip a tall, cool one at the swim-up bar. Stacked stone adorns the planters and the base of the pillars. A custom travertine mosaic forms the border along the swim-up bar and along the pool wall. Patios are finished in travertine. Counters and pool coping is cast concrete in a coordinating color.

On four corners of the pool, square planters hold large fire bowls that distribute warmth and eye candy throughout the yard.

A second outdoor kitchen on the other side of the pool offers extra cooking space during the biggest bashes. When it's not cooking, it provides convenient beverage service.

This yard was featured on HGTV's *Get Out, Way Out!*
Scott Cohen discusses the project with host, Brandon Johnson.

Design Tips :

Light It Right: If you're like most homeowners, you may not have a lot of time to enjoy your outdoor space during the day, so pay close attention to how your landscape will look at night. Lighting was an important part of the planning process in this yard and it shows. The scrolled sconce lights on the pavilion walls, the full-size chandeliers inside, and the fire bowls around the pool all contribute to the nighttime magic.

Replicate and Coordinate: To create a yard that's truly an extension of the home, pull out pleasing architectural elements and building materials from the house and replicate them in the landscape. The Spanish terra cotta tile roof of the pavilion matches the existing architecture of this home.

Have A Seat: Whenever you're adding walls, consider putting them at seat height. You'll thank yourself during your next party. Here the planter walls around the fire bowls provide additional seating when the flames are turned down.

Run The Numbers: When designing a space for entertaining, crunch some numbers to get a realistic look at the space you'll need. How many people do you entertain at your biggest celebrations, your average gatherings, your small dinners? Then plan the furniture, patios, and counter space needed to accommodate these groups. Don't just guess; even a few extra inches in the right place can make a difference.

Exotic Beauty

This sun-drenched landscape blends a bit of Moroccan spice with the poetic grace of a formal Middle Eastern garden.

When the owners of this property envisioned their dream landscape, the woman of the house imagined herself in a tranquil Moroccan escape, while her husband pictured the famed Shalimar Gardens of the couple's Middle Eastern homeland. Both saw a clean green backdrop with bold color accents.

We created a refreshing oasis with a rich emerald lawn that surrounds and traverses the hardscape. A curving, vanishing edge pool takes center stage, accentuating the home's lofty view. Custom hand-painted tile and splashes of red, orange, and yellow glass add warm Moroccan hues to the otherwise neutral palette.

This poolscape received a Best Pool and Spa award at the Western Pool and Spa Show.

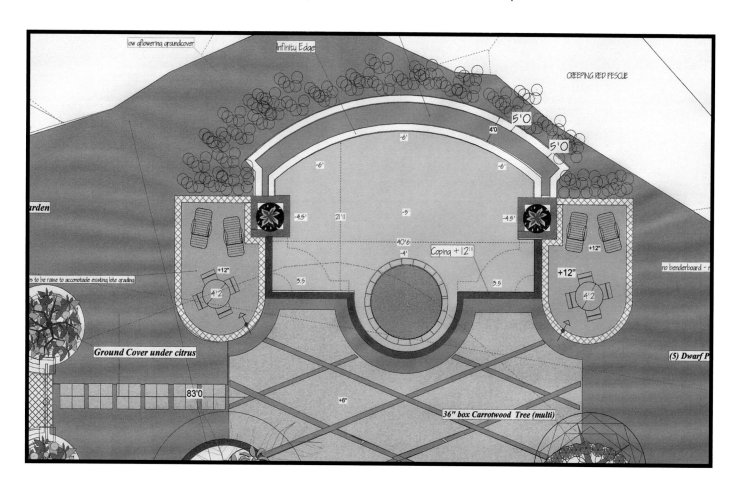

Fetch-A-Sketch.com

With strong geometric shapes, a symmetrical design and an emphasis on water, this landscape borrows a few elements from Paradise Gardens of the Middle East. Identical fire bowls set in large, square planters anchor each side of the vanishing edge, framing the vista, and adding nighttime reflectivity. Two small patios placed symmetrically on either side of the pool offer a place to take in the scene while warming up by the fire.

The U-shaped kitchen counter is designed in two levels for comfortable cooking and bar heights. A fiery red glass tile backsplash divides the two levels. The concrete surface is embedded with crushed red, orange, and yellow recycled glass and is lit from below with 500 fiber-optic cables, which adds nighttime sizzle.

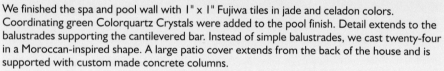

We finished the spa and pool wall with 1" x 1" Fujiwa tiles in jade and celadon colors. Coordinating green Colorquartz Crystals were added to the pool finish. Detail extends to the balustrades supporting the cantilevered bar. Instead of simple balustrades, we cast twenty-four in a Moroccan-inspired shape. A large patio cover extends from the back of the house and is supported with custom made concrete columns.

While the owner loves water, she isn't a confident swimmer, so we designed an oversize spa where she could relax in comfort and security. Like a second outdoor living room, it features a center table where bathers can set their drinks. When it's not needed as a table, its embedded pop-up fountain offers sound and visual entertainment. This project was all about detail. The client was very involved with the color and material selection, and it shows.

Custom Moroccan-inspired tile forms decorative bands around the fire features and along step risers. Each tile is hand-painted and individually glazed.

The spacious central patio is constructed of 3' by 3' square, stamped cast concrete pads crisscrossed by lush greenery. Each pad is roomy enough for a small group to converse in comfort.

The garden includes a formal lily pond encircled by benches and four iron arches. The pond is finished in a blend of hand painted 1" x 1" and 4"x 4" tiles.

Design Tips :

The View Is Everything: Make sure landscaping elements won't interfere with a gorgeous vista. In this project we paid careful attention to placement of hardscape, plants, and trees.

Soften Your Space: Introduce greenery to soften an expansive hardscape. A huge patio like this one could look hard and monotonous without lush greenery to break it up.

A Little Goes A Long Way: Instead of lavishing color everywhere, try using it as an accent. Here, the colorful hand-painted tiles were used only on step risers and key focal points. This gave us high impact from a relatively small amount of an expensive material.

Remember Resale: When you keep your main colors neutral, you'll typically appeal to a greater crowd if you ever decide to sell your home.

Blue Lagoon: A green finish to the pool will give your water that refreshing blue-green tropical hue.

Ouchless Bathing: A pool or spa finished in 1"x1" tiles is much more comfortable on a bikini bottom (or bare bottom) than a pebble or Colorquartz finish. Your skinny-dipping friends will thank you.

Keep Your Eye On The Sky: Watch your skyline colors as you select your plaster or tile pool and spa finishes. This is especially important in a vanishing edge pool where sky tones maximize the illusion.

Sensational
Spas

Sensational Spas

Aaaah … there's nothing like slipping into the warm, soothing bubbles of a spa and feeling your tensions melt away.

For some property owners, a spa alone is actually a more appropriate choice than a pool/spa combo. Some yards are too small to accommodate a pool. Even when there's ample space, many homeowners simply won't use a pool enough to justify the addition.

A spa is less expensive to heat and easier to maintain year-round than a pool. Cold-climate homeowners find that a spa offers a chance to enjoy the outdoors in any season. Soaking in a hot tub under the stars with a glass of wine and some good friends is a delightful way to spend a crisp night.

Regular use of a spa also offers countless health benefits. Physicians and physical therapists often recommend hydrotherapy to improve circulation, reduce blood pressure, soothe sore muscles, and relieve the pain of arthritis and other joint-related conditions.*

As research continues to demonstrate the relationship between stress and illness, the importance of taking time to relax each and every day becomes more apparent. Think of a spa as your prescription for relaxation.

Today's spas aren't just for soaking. With swim jets that enable users to paddle against a current, a spa can actually serve as an exercise pool. Underwater weight sets, resistance bands, and other accessories can turn your spa into an invigorating outdoor setting for a high power, low impact workout.

There are many types of spas available including custom in-ground units, above-ground acrylic spas, and wooden hot tubs. There are even some new portable spas. While these have limitations, they can be appropriate in some yards.

With or without a full-size pool, a creatively designed spa can add a spectacular waterscape to your backyard. From a naturalistic pond, to a pristine reflecting pool, to an old world fountain, a uniquely landscaped spa can take on a look or feel to complement any home.

In the following pages we'll share some of our best design secrets for creating sensational backyard spa retreats.

Vanishing Edge Vista

You don't need a full-size pool to add vanishing edge drama to your backyard.

These homeowners didn't need a swimming pool, but they wanted a spa and loved the look of the infinity edge illusion. We created this vanishing edge pond to accentuate the home's hillside view. We added a generous spa with another illusion: a rushing waterfall that appears to flow from pond to spa. It's actually fed by a water feature embedded in the cast concrete bridge.

We built this pond for a fraction of the cost it would take to construct a vanishing edge pool.

While creating the illusion of a stream, the 8' waterfall actually recirculates spa water for an over-the-shoulder heated massage.

The faux wood footbridge leads to a small viewing patio with a stamped cast concrete surface.

Fetch-A-Sketch.com

The pond is actually an active fish pond where the homeowners keep 15-20 pet coy. (There's always at least one black one for good luck.)

Low growing plantings add naturalistic appeal around the pond while keeping the view open.

The pond offers the full-reflectivity of a vanishing edge, perfectly capturing the changing view. The owners enjoy magical sunrises from their east-facing yard.

A River Runs Through It

A small stream wanders through this yard, ending in a rocky waterfall that spills into a generous, custom-tile spa.

The owners of this Santa Barbara home thoroughly embrace Feng Shui concepts. The road leading to their property approaches the home from behind and this creates bad chi. Flowing water can correct this negative energy, so we created a long, narrow brook running through the yard along a back patio.

A footbridge crosses the stream to a cozy fire-pit with a semi-circle stone seat wall. This combination protects the home with fire and water.

The flagstone hardscape and field stone boulders add a rustic, earthy feel.

A custom copper gate leads from backyard to the side yard where the spa is located.

The spa is 14' long by 8' at its widest point. It includes 12 hydrotherapy jets along with swim jets for exercising against the current. The walls are adorned with a custom fish tile mosaic created by Michelle Griffoul studios.

Lush plantings enclose the yard, creating an intimate sanctuary.

At the end of the project, a Feng Shui master walked the landscape and gave full approval to the design.

Relax and Rejuvenate

Water flows from a trio of fountains into a spacious spa below.

The owners of this smaller backyard wanted a striking focal point for their landscape along with the health benefits of hydrotherapy. This spa, with its custom tile backsplash, makes a stunning water feature on its own. When in use, the flowing water provides heated therapeutic massage.

The tall backsplash does double duty as a retaining wall. This enables us to carve into the slope, adding more usable space to this small yard.

Two sheer spillways flank a center sun medallion. The neutral expanse of blue tile with a matte finish is deigned to pick up the color of the water. A custom grapevine mosaic from the studios of Michelle Griffoul trims the bias-set tile. While custom tile work is quite expensive, using it as an accent makes an artistic touch like this more affordable.

A wood pergola extends over patio and spa to shade bathers in this sunny yard.

The adjacent outdoor kitchen includes a matching backsplash.

The patio surface is stamped cast concrete. Coping is cast concrete with a bull-nose edge.

Custom tiles by my good friend and tile artist Michelle Griffoul - MichelleGriffoul.com

A Toast to The Vine

This spa pours forth a joyful, colorful, and whimsical celebration of all the gifts of the vine.

We crafted this unique water feature for some wine enthusiast friends. They frequently host wine-tasting events and wanted an entertaining backyard where they could savor their hobby in style.

We built a Napa-themed spa/fountain using 450 colored wine bottles. Five hundred fiber-optic cables feed the feature from behind while a sparkler wheel sets the subtly colored lights in motion. The effect is mesmerizing right from the first toast, and … well, it just keeps getting better as the evening unfolds.

Our structural engineer told us the wine bottle wall has the strength of glass block construction … but it's a lot more fun.

The 14' x 5' wall is flanked by two concrete pilasters adorned with tiles I created in my home kiln especially for the clients. I designed the 3-D vine motif using castings made from actual wine bottles.

Three waterfall weirs are embedded among the bottles. The color of the falling water slowly changes as the sparkler wheel rotates.

An adjacent fire-pit with a seat-wall and lamppost creates a large outdoor room where guests in and out of the spa can compare notes on their favorite vintages.

Before adding the spa, the homeowners looked out on a large expanse of wall. Now the colorful fountain breaks up the wall and adds a striking focal point to the yard.

This spa was featured on HGTV's "Big Splash," a special highlighting some of the country's most spectacular pools and spas.

Old California Vista

This Spanish Mission style spa terrace offers an optimal spot for enjoying panoramic sky and valley views.

The property's downward slope creates a magnificent vista, but it also poses some construction challenges. The owners wanted a large spa and functional outdoor rooms with an Old California look. To make sure these new features stayed put, we anchored them to the yard with a low retaining wall that extends six feet into the ground. The wall also creates an ideal spot for a water feature.

Water pours into the spa from six terra cotta clay drain pipes for a unique fountain that also offers a warm massage.

The water is back-fed with fiber optic cables that light the streams of water at night.

A permanent shade structure over the nearby step-up outdoor kitchen keeps the cook cool and comfortable.

The warm hues of this hardscape help create the old Spanish Mission feel. The terra cotta stamped concrete deck and the cast concrete coping in a sandstone color coordinate with the outdoor kitchen's Salito tile flooring.

The walls of the generously sized rectangular fire pit are finished with hand-painted Mexican Talavera tiles. This accents the earth-toned palette with a festive punch of color.

We placed the fire against the low wall at the edge of the property, so owners and their guests can take full advantage of the home's forever view.

Fetch-A-Sketch.com

Water Features

Water Features

As you've probably guessed by now, I'm wild about water features. A well-designed pool or spa is beautiful on its own, but when you accent it with a fountain, a waterfall or another flowing work of art, you can create a true backyard masterpiece.

Water in motion adds tremendous entertainment value to the landscape. The same fountain that gives the water park amusement for kids by day creates romantic ambiance for adults after dark. Some features provide a warm soothing massage in the spa. Others offer a cooling spray to hot sunbathers.

Running water helps set the tone for a backyard. The pleasant sound it makes as it falls hushes traffic and quiets neighborhood noise. With the addition of color and light, water can create a dazzling nighttime show that takes backyard entertaining to a new level.

It may surprise you to know that the many custom-crafted water features shown in this book are created with just a few different fixtures used in a variety of different applications. With a little creativity and the right combination of products, you can customize your pool or spa with a natural looking stream, a bubbling old world fountain, a glassy modernistic sheet of water or an infinite array of other options.

Here are some of the fixtures and methods I like best:

Sheer Cascade or Sheet Waterfall (bottom pg. 140) – This type of waterfall, also known as a Sheer Descent, is available under different proprietary names, and produces a clean, glossy sheet of water. Sheet falls come in straight or curving models in a variety of lengths up to eight feet. They can also be custom-fabricated to meet specific design needs. Commonly made of white PVC or colored plastic, these are now available in copper, stainless steel, and other metal finishes.

Fiber optic lighting installed below the fixture can greatly enhance this type of waterfall. The sheet of water carries the unbroken light for about three feet before gravity scatters the water into tiny droplets. The effect is subtle and elegant.

A sheer cascade can also provide a heated water massage with re-circulated spa water.

Sheer Rainfall (right) – Instead of a single sheet of water, this feature produces a showering curtain of droplets. Sheer rainfalls are an especially good option when the feature will be placed high above the pool or spa. (When water falls from greater heights, the effect of a sheet-type water feature is lost as gravity pulls the sheet apart before it reaches viewing level). Like the sheer cascade, a sheer rainfall is also used for water massage and is very comfortable to sit beneath.

Weir Waterfall (bottom left) – Sometimes the spa is set at a higher elevation than the pool. You can construct a narrow outlet or weir to create a gentle cascade that directs the flow naturally from spa to pool or from one water feature to another. Pre-made weirs are available in copper, stainless steel, and tile. We also carve our own out of stone for an extra special look.

Medallion stream (below) – This spout of water emerges from a decorative wall medallion. Typically plumbed with half-inch pipe, medallion fountains are available in shapes and materials to suit a wide variety of themes or styles. They're a great way to add interesting detail to any poolscape.

Deck Jets (above) – This adjustable feature is mounted flush outside the coping around the perimeter of a pool. It produces a narrow arcing stream of water that shoots into the pool from a hole in the concrete. With adjustable nozzles, you can change the distance and height of the spout to create different effects. Deck jets are easy to install and offer a relatively inexpensive way to turn any pool or spa into an eye-catching fountain.

Laminar Jets (below) – Like a deck jet, this classy feature shoots a narrow stream of water but with a dramatic difference. As it emerges, the pristine water holds its shape, creating the illusion of a solid rod of clear glass or acrylic. Laminar jets can be used singly or in groups for very interesting "architectural" effects. Illumination adds to the drama as light is carried flawlessly through the entire stream.

Laminar jets are best suited to sites that aren't frequently disturbed by wind. Even a moderate breeze can shatter the illusion, so to speak, so in windy spots, less expensive deck jet may be more appropriate.

Telescoping Pool Fountain (below) – Also called a pop-up fountain, this feature is installed in the pool shell. When not in use, the fountain sits flush with the pool floor where it won't pose a tripping hazard to swimmers. When it's turned on, hydraulic pressure extends the nozzle and a beautiful fountain emerges. I like to place these in a Baja shelf to cool down sunbathers or create a fun play area for little ones.

Telescoping fountains are available in a number of spray and foaming patterns. All can be illuminated for extra after dark entertainment. One of my favorite nighttime features is the "shower of diamonds" display of illuminated fountain droplets scattering on the pool surface. It's pure magic.

Sculptural Fountain (below) – Sculptural garden fountains are available in bronze, stone, cast concrete, resin, fiberglass, and other materials. When used adjacent to the pool they can be plumbed to re-circulate pool water.

A sculptural piece is a great way to add a unique and interesting focal point to your poolscape. It can expand on your theme and reflect your own personal artistic style.

Urns, Bowls, or Scupper Fountains (below) – Large pots and open bowls or basins make gorgeous water features. They're available in cast concrete, stone, or metal, including bronze, copper, and stainless. Some have a pouring lip or scupper built into the rim to direct flowing water

Container fountains are typically plumbed from the bottom with re-circulated water that spills back into the pool. You can keep the pipe open for an even flow or add a nozzle for a special display like the foaming effect shown here.

Some bowls and scupper fountains are also available with a fire feature option. This allows you to easily combine fire and water in the same piece.

Precast concrete scuppers are reminiscent of old world water features. The reflection on the illusion spa is created by using a slot overflow, overflowing on all sides of the spa. On the back side, water spills into a 1/4" wide slot and is collected by a drainage channel.

Water Feature Tips :

A Feature for Every Home – Water features are a great way to expand on a theme. Make sure the features you choose fit the style of your overall poolscape. With countless options to choose from, it's easy to find one that harmonizes with your look.

Control the Action – Sometimes silence is golden. Include a manual valve for your feature so you can turn it on and off or adjust the flow to fit the mood.

Individual Operation – If you have more than one water feature, consider independent valves so you can adjust the flow to each one separately. Maximum water flow in one feature might produce a pleasing stream while in another it could create a firehose-like blast.

Get Loopy – Sometimes it makes sense to install multiple water features along a single line, such as a row of deck jets on the side of the pool. When you do, be sure to loop the plumbing so you'll have uniform water pressure to each feature. If you don't, the feature closest to the pump will see all the action while the one at the end will droop.

Don't Shock Your Guests! – Refer to local ordinances when installing metal fountains or sculptures within the pool or spa area. Make sure a qualified electrician is involved with your project.

The perimeter overflow spa captures views on the horizon. Darker tiles enhance the reflective quality. The darker the tile, the more reflective the quality.

Photo by Marie G. Nuzzi

Top 10 Plants For Pools

Creating a beautiful garden oasis around a swimming pool has several interesting challenges. You want plantings to be colorful and lush, reflecting the ambience of the water they surround, but you don't want litter to blow into the pool, causing frequent maintenance that requires a lot of hand skimming and filter cleaning. For these reasons, the designers at The Green Scene select varieties of plants that satisfy the need for cleanliness and are also luxuriant, colorful, and look great around a swimming pool.

A tropical plant pallet is ideal for enhancing the relaxed feel of the pool area and decking. Palm trees like the Queen Palm (Syagrus romanzoffianum) gently sway in the breeze and create a light, filtered shade below. The shorter Pigmy Date Palm (Phoenix roebelenii) and the Sago Palm (Cycas revoluta) are perfect specimens for adding interest. With its ultra long stems with hairy green pom-poms, the Papyrus (Cyperus papyrus) also provides interest and a good background to other tropical plants like Bird of Paradise (Strelitzia reginae), Fortnight Lily (Dietes vegeta), and the classic plant associated with Hawaii – the Hibiscus (Hibiscus sinensis) pictured above.

Not only perfect for a tropical setting, the following plants can readily cross over into other design schemes, adding foundation and clean, brilliant color with their foliage instead of their flowers. Red Tip Photinia (Photinia fraseri) and Heavenly bamboo (Nandina domestica), which is not a real bamboo nor invasive, both add a rusty red to the garden and both make a good background or screen. A dwarf variety (N. domestica 'Nana Compacta') can be used as a border plant or even as a groundcover. Golden Euonymus (Euonymus japonica 'Aureo-variegata') and Gold Dust Plant (Aucuba japonica) brighten up the planting with yellow variegated foliage. The strappy leaves of New Zealand Flax (Phormium tenax) comes in a variety of colors, as do many types of grasses.

There are lots of smaller perennials (plants that do not die after flowering) that can add plenty of continuous color without creating a mess. As the flowers die off, they stay on the plant until clipped off, keeping them out of the pool. Day Lily (Hemerocalis hybrid) (below center), Lily of the Nile (Agapanthus Africanas), (below left), the dwarf version 'Peter Pan', Alstroemaria and Sea Lavender (Limonium perezii) will all perform well with minimum maintenance.

Seasonal color annuals get the job done too. Pansy (above right), Lobelia, Marigold, Blue Salvia and many others can liven up a space with fast growing, bright color without dropping their petals, allowing you to spend your time relaxing by the pool instead of cleaning it!

Foreground: Carrotwood tree, groundcovers of "Pink Thrift" Armeria, Red Verbena, and bronze "Coral Bells" Heuchera
Background: "Sea Lavender" Limonium perezii, "Foxtail Fern" Asparagus meyerii, "Purple Hopseed" Dodonaea viscosa, and Mayten trees

Pool Construction 101

Here's a brief overview of the steps involved in the typical pool construction process. This section is intended to give homeowners an idea of what to expect at each of the main steps of building an in-ground concrete (gunite or shotcrete) pool. This chapter is not intended to be relied upon as a pool building manual.

Your pool building experience will be more fun and exciting once you understand the common trade terms and lingo used by the folks in the biz. You will also be able to better communicate with your pool contractor or water feature designer.

Pool shell installation with gunite

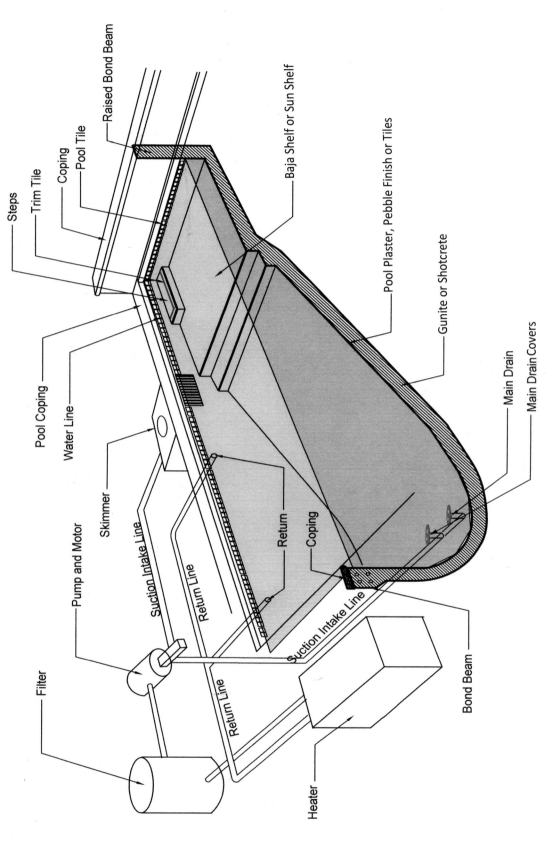

Parts of a Typical Pool

Steps

Trim Tile

Coping

Pool Tile

Raised Bond Beam

Pool Coping

Water Line

Skimmer

Pump and Motor

Suction Intake Line

Return Line

Return

Coping

Suction Intake Line

Return Line

Filter

Heater

Bond Beam

Baja Shelf or Sun Shelf

Pool Plaster, Pebble Finish or Tiles

Gunite or Shotcrete

Main Drain

Main Drain Covers

Plans, Permits, Soils Reports, and Engineering:

Each community across the U.S. seems to have its own set of rules regarding pool construction, or in some cases, no rules at all. Even when permits are not required, I always recommend you obtain the services of a structural engineer experienced with swimming pool construction to design your pool shell. Consultation with a soils geologist is strongly recommended in sloped areas and when unique soils conditions exist. Be wary of contractors willing to perform work without a permit if one is typically required in your community.

Site Layout:

In order to better visualize your yard, the pool and garden design should be laid out on the ground using marking paint or chalk (baking flour works just fine too). This allows you to confirm location, size, and features with your construction contractor before the hole is dug. Changes made in the paint-out stage are always less expensive than after the pool hole is excavated. At this time it is a good idea to confirm pool depths and step and bench locations with your builder.

Excavation:

The pool excavator will first set wooden forms and stakes to match the shape of the swimming vessel and set the top heights of the pool shell. Once forms are set, the digging begins with the help of a tractor, or backhoe, but can be hand dug where access is very limited.

The excavation process typically takes 2-5 days depending on soils conditions, weather, and the complexity of your pool design.

At this stage, sometimes home-owners express concern that the pool will be too large. Please note that the dirt hole is being over-dug in size to accommodate steel and gunite placement. Your actual pool will be smaller than the excavated hole by about one foot all the way around.

Steel Reinforcement:

A cage of "*rebar,*" deformed bumpy bars of steel reinforcement, will be set following the structural engineer's instructions. The intersections of the steel grid will be tied with wire, called "*tie-wires,*" to strengthen the shell cage. "*Dobies,*" or block spacers, will be set between the steel cage and the soil to leave a space for the concrete and to keep the steel in the center of the concrete shell. At the very top edge of the steel shell, extra pieces of rebar steel will be tied to form a "*bond beam,*" the very top portion of the pool that ties the whole structure together.

Plumbing:

PVC pipes are run from the pre-determined pool equipment area to the pool and spa shell for water circulation, water features, skimmers, and main drains. Gas pipes are run from the equipment area to the main gas service at the home (unless propane or electric heaters are utilized). Stub outs for solar panels are installed at this time.

Plumbing pipes should be "*looped*" at the equipment and pressurized to ensure there are no leaks. Professional plumbers will install a valve at the equipment area for monitoring throughout the construction process. If pressure drops on the valve, stop all construction until the leak can be located and repaired. Plumbing loops will be cut down at the time your pool equipment is installed.

Electrical:

Initially called "*rough electrical,*" the first step in the electrical system construction process is to get all conduits (pipes that protect interior wiring) in place. PVC or metal pipes are run from the home's main electrical panel to the pool equipment area, then to the pool lighting niches and other electrical outlet locations planned in the yard. At this time conduits for hard-wired remote control systems and spa side switches are run.

Later, after the pool shell gunite has been placed, the electrician will return to your site to pull wires through the conduits, wire the pumps, heaters and other equipment, and connect remote control systems.

Gunite or Shotcrete:

In-ground concrete pools are typically "shot" in place using either "gunite" or "shotcrete" concrete placement methods. Gunite is a combination of sand and cement mixed at the construction site and shot dry through a hose as water is added at the very end of the hose nozzle. Shotcrete is a mixture of sand, cement, and aggregate and is shipped pre-mixed wet to the site and applied at

pressure onto the pool walls. Your contractor will select either of these placement methods depending on local soils conditions and recommendations made by your structural engineer. This concrete placement process provides the structural part of the pool shell and it is completely porous (does not hold water). Plastering is required to coat the concrete and provide the waterproof qualities of the swimming pool.

Pool Engineering Source

Pool Engineering Inc's Ron Lacher is my structural engineer and a respected leader in the pool and spa industry. He teaches seminars nationally on proper pool construction techniques. Mr. Lacher runs Pool Engineering Inc., a structural engineering and design firm in sunny California, but serves most of the United States. www.pooleng.com

What is "*rock time*"?

Pool Contractors quote excavation work assuming soils removal with a standard tractor. At times during excavation harder bedrock, rocks or boulders may be found in the area intended to be the pool. Excavators are entitled to charge additional fees to remove these rocks and boulders using heavy-duty demolition hammer equipment. Be sure you have an understanding with your pool contractor in advance on how "rock-time" is billed should it be encountered during construction of your project.

Why do you have to water a pool shell immediately after it has been installed?

Both gunite and shotcrete are installed with very little water in the mixture. In order for the concrete to cure to the full strength intended, proper hydration of the cement must occur. Apply water thoroughly to your pool shell 4-5 times per day for a period of 7-10 days to ensure a complete and proper cure. Some contractors will aid in this wetting process by supplementing hand watering with soaker hoses and temporary sprinkler systems. This wetting process is extremely important to the long term performance of your pool shell.

A word of caution about salt chlorine generators and pool coping: A current popular trend is to use a salt chlorine generator and add salt crystals to the pool water instead of standard chlorine. Salt system treated water is easier on the eyes and helps soften your skin. Salted pool water has only a slightly salty taste and many folks prefer water treated this way in lieu of chlorine tablets. Please be aware though that pool water treated with salt systems will build up mineral crystals inside porous pool coping and speed the demise of the coping product. In the course of performing construction defect expert witness consultations, I have seen stone pool coping literally dissolve (prematurely) from excessive salt water exposure. If you plan to use a salt system, be sure to select a pool coping material that is less porous and routinely wash your decks and coping with fresh water.

Coping:

The decorative cap that is placed on top of the bond beam is referred to as coping. Many choices are available including stone, ledge-stone, bricks, cast concrete, pre-cast concrete, and tile. Coping can be placed before or after waterline tile depending on the preferred installation method of your contractor.

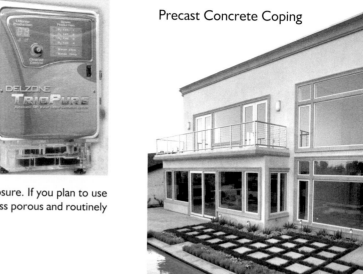

Precast Concrete Coping

Photo by Jim Jordan

Ledgestone Coping

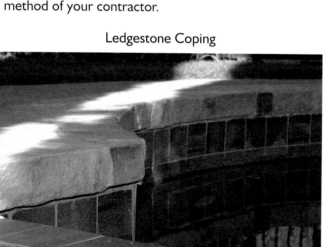

Travertine Coping

Cast In Place Concrete Coping

Brick Coping

Tile:

The "waterline," or "scum-line" (the very top surface of the water level), of a pool shell is tiled to ease maintenance and maintain the waterproof properties of the swimming pool or spa. Plaster finishes cannot be used in a wet-dry-wet environment, so tile is required. Tiles can be ceramic or glass and are available in thousands of different patterns and colors. I always advise clients to select tiles that they believe will be timeless so they don't date a pool by choosing a time-trendy product. A word of caution: I have seen authentic stone tiles used in submerged and waterline applications dissolve quickly from the corrosive properties of water, so my recommendation is to stick to ceramic and glass tiles and avoid using stone in submerged applications.

Interior Finishes:

Swimming pool interior finishes provide the waterproof layer of the swimming pool. Plasters are available in a multitude of colors and textures including, smooth

marble, colored quarts chips, mini-pebbles, glass beads, and polished pebbles. Ceramic or glass tiles can also be used to coat the entire interior of the pool when proper waterproof coatings are used substrate.

Start-Up:

Just add water! Once the water is added to your pool a "start-up" process must be followed to properly cure the interior finish. This start-up process will vary depending on the product selected for the interior finish. It is important that the pool fill quickly and water not be turned off until the pool is completely filled. Failure to fill the pool all at once can create a "ring" on the pool walls that can't be easily removed. Verify that your pool contractor will provide the first week of start-up and pool maintenance. Thereafter, the responsibility for water chemistry will likely be turned over to you or your pool maintenance serviceman.

What is "Bonding"?

Copper wires may be run to "*bond*" all metal materials within five feet of the pool shell. "*Bonding*" is the permanent joining of metallic parts to form an electrically conductive path that ensures electrical continuity and the capacity to conduct safely any current likely to be imposed. Creating an electrically safe environment in and around permanently installed swimming pools requires the installation of a bonding system with the sole function of establishing equal electrical potential (voltage) in the vicinity of the swimming pool. A person who is immersed in a pool or who is dripping wet, has a large amount of exposed skin, and who is lying or walking on a concrete deck is extremely susceptible to any differences in electrical potential that may be present in the pool area.

The primary purpose of bonding in and around swimming pools is to ensure that voltage gradients in the pool area are not present. The reason for connecting metal parts (ladders, handrails, water-circulating equipment, forming shells, diving boards, etc.) to a common bonding grid, like the pool reinforcing steel, is to ensure that all such metal parts are at the same electrical potential. The grid reduces possible injurious or disabling shock hazards created by stray currents in the ground or piping connected to the swimming pool.

Glossary

Here are a few pool and spa terms that might come in handy when you're talking with your designer or builder.

Baja Shelf/ Sun Shelf – A level, shallow area in the pool that provides a comfortable spot for sunbathing. It can also serve as a shallow play area for small children.

Bond Beam – The top portion of a pool wall. A raised bond beam refers to one that is elevated above the other pool walls. This can also serve as a retaining wall for holding back soil when the pool is built into a slope.

Coping – The top surface of the bond beam that provides a finished edge to the pool. It can be created from concrete, brick, tile, stone, and other decorative materials.

Concrete – A mixture of sand, portland cement and water that can be pre-cast or cast-in-place for use in several different applications in and around the pool and spa. Concrete is often stamped, colored, and/or embedded with decorative aggregates to achieve an infinite variety of decorative looks and textures.

Concrete Pavers – Pre-cast concrete units used to create patios, walkways, and pool/spa decks. Units are often tumbled, colored, and molded in an assortment of shapes and sizes to coordinate with diverse styles.

Deck – The area immediately around the pool or spa outside of the coping. It can be finished with cast concrete, concrete pavers, stone, brick, wood decking and other materials. A pool engineered with a "zero deck detail" allows vegetation right up to the pool coping.

Deep-Well Spa – A spa deep enough for two or more adults to stand in. It's a great choice for hydrotherapy spas and romantic backyard retreats.

Flagstone – Large flat slabs of stone suitable for pool coping, decking, patios, and walkways. Irregularly shaped pieces add a more natural, rustic look to the landscape.

Hardscape – The hard, non-vegetated, portion of the landscape, including the pavement, walls, pillars, counters, etc.

Hydrotherapy – The use of flowing, heated water for relaxation and therapeutic massage. With the variety of jets and waterfalls available today, a number of different hydrotherapy treatments can be incorporated into the spa or pool.

Infinity Pool/Vanishing Edge Pool – Also called an "illusion edge" or "negative edge," this pool or spa treatment gives the illusion that water extends infinitely to the horizon. In reality, a thin layer of water continuously flows over the edge into a catch basin below. This creates a highly reflective surface and a beautiful horizon line that's especially striking in yards with an expansive view or in properties overlooking water.

Lap Pool – A pool long enough and deep enough to provide a straight-line distance adequate for swimming exercise.

Main Drain – A drain located at the deepest end of the pool. Drain line covers should be split with two suctions set a minimum of three feet apart and have anti-entrapment covers placed over openings.

Mastic Joint – A urethane sealant that is placed between the pool deck/hardscape and the pool coping material. The sealant is placed above a layer of silica sand or foam. Pool mastic is used to create an expansion joint allowing decks and pools to move independently and avoid damage to pool coping or concrete. Mastic is available in a variety of different colors.

Palapa – An open-sided structure with a thatched roof. It is sometimes used to provide permanent shade around a tropical themed pool.

Pergola – An outdoor structure with a slatted or trelliswork roof and/or sides that supports vining plants. It can be used for shade around the pool.

Pebble Finish – An alternative to the traditional smooth plaster pool finish. A wide variety of pebble finishes are available to add dramatic color, texture, or sparkle to the pool.

Plaster Finish – A traditional smooth waterproof finish applied to the inside of the pool. It can be white or colored in various shades. Numerous additives such as 3M Colorquartz crystals can offer different textures and add richer shades of variegated color.

Ramada – A semi-open, roofed outdoor room that can be used for shade around the landscape.

Seat Wall – A retaining wall or decorative wall built at a height comfortable for sitting. Seat walls are a great way to define a space while adding extra seating at the same time.

Shotcrete/Gunite – Shotcrete is a spray-on type of concrete that is used to create the shell of a pool or spa. It is applied using a hose. It can also be used to create waterfalls, rocks, slides, etc. Gunite is the name for a special dry-mix type of shotcrete. Water is only added at the end of the hose. The words are often used interchangeably.

Skimmer – A device installed in the wall of the pool that is connected to the suction line of the pump. The suction pulls in water and floating contaminants which are collected in a skimmer basket. Skimmers perform best when placed on the prevailing downwind side of the pool so that wind blows debris toward the skimmer.

Slate – A fine grained, metamorphic rock that splits into thin, smooth layers. It's often cut into regular square or rectangular pieces for use as pool coping, decking, patios, and walkways. It's suitable for both naturalistic and modern looking landscapes.

Swim Jet – A system that can be installed in a pool or spa to create a continuous current for treadmill-type swimming exercise. This is a popular way to turn a spa or smaller pool into a "lap pool."

Tile Finish – Another alternative to the traditional smooth plaster finish. An all-tile finish offers countless options for adding jewel-like color and artistic flair to the pool. A smooth tile finish is also a bit friendlier on sensitive bare skin!

Travertine – A porous natural sedimentary stone often used for pool/spa decking, patios, walls, and other building projects. Its rough porous texture and warm earth tones blend well with Tuscan and other old-world styles.

Trim Tile – A row of tile set at the edge of a step to improve visibility for safety. Typically a row or two of 1x1 tile in a color other than the pool interior finish.

Water Feature – A decorative landscaping element designed around flowing water. Fountains, water spouts, waterfalls, and cascades can all add a higher level of beauty and fun to the poolscape.

Waterline Tile – A row of tile set directly below the coping and placed so that the top water level runs across the middle of the tile. Typically a six inch row of tile is set at the waterline. Waterline tile is necessary because plaster finishes do not perform well in an alternating wet/dry environment. Waterline tile also aids maintenance and cleaning of the "scum line."

Zero Entry/Beach Entry – A very gradual entry to the shallow end of a pool. This treatment is popular in pools used by small children. Gradual entry can also be achieved with a sun shelf/Baja shelf. This offers the extra advantage of a level surface for lounging.